The Irrepressible Mary Jeune, Victorian Influencer

The Irrepressible
Mary Jeune,
Victorian Influencer

AMELIA FLETCHER

Copyright © 2025 Amelia Fletcher

The moral right of the author has been asserted.

Apart from any fair dealing for the purposes of research or private study, or criticism or review, as permitted under the Copyright, Designs and Patents Act 1988, this publication may only be reproduced, stored or transmitted, in any form or by any means, with the prior permission in writing of the publishers, or in the case of reprographic reproduction in accordance with the terms of licences issued by the Copyright Licensing Agency. Enquiries concerning reproduction outside those terms should be sent to the publishers.

Troubador Publishing Ltd
Unit E2 Airfield Business Park
Harrison Road, Market Harborough
Leicestershire LE16 7UL
Tel: 0116 279 2299
Email: books@troubador.co.uk
Web: www.troubador.co.uk

ISBN 978 1 83628 391 1

British Library Cataloguing in Publication Data.
A catalogue record for this book is available from the British Library.

The manufacturer's authorised representative in the EU for product safety is Authorised Rep Compliance Ltd, 71 Lower Baggot Street, Dublin D02 P593 Ireland (www.arccompliance.com).

Printed and bound in Great Britain by 4edge Limited
Typeset in 11pt Jenson Pro by Troubador Publishing Ltd, Leicester, UK

This book is dedicated to all Mary Jeune's descendants

Contents

Introducing Mary Jeune   xi

A Hostess of Genius   1
*In which Mary throws the doors of Society
wide open and lets in an invigorating breeze*

Extravagance in Dress   7
*In which Mary's parents (and the spiritual domination
of the Free Church of Scotland) leave her with a lifetime's
aversion to extravagance of any kind*

London in the Sixties   17
*In which Mary has her education broadened
by two uncompromising women*

The Stanleys of Alderley   25
*In which Mary marries into a family famed for
its bad behaviour as much as for its brilliance*

Not for the Faint-hearted   39
*In which Mary's marriage to Johnny Stanley involves a Wild
West adventure, and saddling her daughters with men's names*

Flirting with Socialism   47
*In which Mary is admired for the 'width of her sympathies'
as revolutionaries flock to her drawing room*

Francis Jeune   55
In which Mary finds happiness in her second marriage

Slumming 63
In which Mary teams up with an ex-pirate, hunts down slum landlords and mounts a landmark prosecution

The Theatre and Millicent Fawcett 75
In which Mary enjoys a very public disagreement with Millicent and her Social Purity vigilantes – but makes it up over Suffrage

The Real Lady Bracknell? 85
In which Mary collaborates with Oscar Wilde and inspires some of his best lines

Two sides of the Irish Question 97
In which Mary keeps a foot firmly in both camps, and does what she can to find an answer

Black Lives Matter 108
In which Mary invites a civil rights activist to have tea with her and the children

An Unreliable Witness 114
In which Mary provides fruitful connections for Frank Harris and abundant material for his memoirs

The New Woman and the Bicycle 121
In which Mary doubts that New Woman is the 'most brilliant development of this most original age', although the bicycle definitely is

Mary Jeune's Dosser 135
In which Mary provides a bolt-hole for Thomas Hardy and an escape from Emma, while he becomes Uncle Tom to her daughters

Mujeres Tuercas	144
In which Mary falls in (and out?) of love with the automobile	
Omdurman and After	150
In which Mary gives Winston Churchill a leg-up and shows her loyalty for a fallen hero	
Undue Influence	158
In which questions are asked about the power behind the scenes	
A Great Venue for a Wedding Breakfast	164
In which Mary makes sure her new house is not a waste of space	
Widowhood and Work	170
In which Mary shows that there's no need to be useless just because you're a Lady	
The Meteoric Career of Billy Bishop	180
In which Mary 'adopts' a Canadian airman and helps him to cheat his way to the top	
Epilogue	189
In which I come across an unexpected connection in a Berkshire village	
Appendix: The Curse of the Mackenzies	196
A Succession of Females	201
Bibliography	202
Acknowledgements	207
Picture Credits	208

Introducing Mary Jeune[1]

I never meant to write a book about my great-great-grandmother. All I had in mind was a slender volume aimed at any family members who might one day be curious about their remarkable ancestor. My idea was to take Mary Jeune's own memoir, select some of the best stories, and translate them from her stiff Victorian style into something more easily digestible for a generation who finds it hard to focus for long on anything other than a screen.

I was handicapped by the lack of any personal letters (Mary admits to a habit of 'consigning correspondence to the flames'). She didn't keep a diary; I don't think she had time. So I turned to that cornucopia of information which is the internet – with startling results. Mary Jeune's name turned up all over the place: in reminiscences by her contemporaries, in (mainly American) learned papers, and in contemporary newspaper reports. Heather Weaver, an American academic, goes so far as to compare her to Lady Di, a woman constantly pursued by paparazzi and reported on in newspapers on both sides of the Atlantic. And yet she has vanished from history.

It became clear that this was a person who deserved a wider audience than the modest number of her descendants who survived the ravages of illness, war, and the family curse. I realised that a book was the only way to do justice to her many accomplishments, and that much harder than finding material to include was going to be deciding what to leave out. Before I go any further I must acknowledge the vital help and support I received from my sister, who helped me to scour the world wide web and offered

---

1   Jeune is pronounced *'June'*

encouragement at every moment when I felt the task getting on top of me. Thank you, Camilla.

A shortage of written evidence was not the only handicap I faced. Having spent most of my life trying to flee from my privileged background, I thought it would be hard to sustain enthusiasm for such a very staunch pillar of the establishment as my great-great-grandma appeared to be. I needn't have worried. My research soon began to reveal aspects of her life that are given no hint in her own memoir. Although famous in her time as a 'Leader of Society', Mary Jeune was much, much more than a society hostess. From her position of privilege she championed the poor and lambasted the rich. She used her connections to influence those at the top, and to give a leg-up to those who struggled below. I was astounded by her fearlessness and her inexhaustible energy – at the same time I frequently found myself chuckling at the absurd contradictions that the competing interests of her life threw up.

As one reviewer commented at the time, Mary's own book, *Memories of Fifty Years*, 'errs on the side of caution'. Gossipy revelations are few and far between, while many colourful characters have been omitted altogether. Her own sense of decorum could have been partly to blame – after all, when the book appeared many of the notables she mentions were still alive. But she was clearly aware that her finished product might make for rather dull reading, for in the introduction she offers this lament:

> a feeling almost of despair arises as one realises how much the interest of one's book is curtailed by the elimination of so much which, for obvious reasons, could not now be published.

Well now it can! I like to think of this book as a companion volume to hers, one in which the 'eliminated' elements are reinstated. Her friendship and collaboration with Oscar Wilde, for example, could not be mentioned. I discovered that she had dealings with many rogues, eccentrics and outcasts: Henry Hyndman, founder of Britain's first socialist party. Bennett Burleigh, pirate and war correspondent. Henry Stanley, Britain's first Muslim peer. Lady Colin Campbell, victim of the sleaziest divorce case of the century. Frank Harris, salacious pioneer of tabloid sensationalism. And more...

In the course of her long life Mary went through many incarnations. She entered the world in 1845 as Mary Stewart Mackenzie, became a Stanley by marriage, became Mrs Jeune at her second marriage, and ended her days as Lady St Helier, due to her second husband's ennoblement. This can be confusing, so while I refer to her throughout as simple 'Mary', I will help the reader with reminders along the way.

A Hostess of Genius

*In which Mary throws the doors of Society wide
open and lets in an invigorating breeze*

When Mary Jeune died, in 1931, her obituaries harked back to her heyday at the end of the previous century – she was, they said, a 'hostess of genius'. By then the very notion of a society hostess was sounding old-fashioned. It conjures up a picture of someone rich and glamorous, flamboyant even. Mary was none of these things – photographs of her at any age show a respectable matron buttoned tightly up in clothing that verges on the puritanical.

How then, in the 1890s, did she manage to be so famous – for she was – as the very lynchpin of London society? How did she progress from arriving in London at the age of 18, with neither title nor fortune, to become one of the most influential women of the period? What was it that made people vie for invitations to her house in Marylebone, where they would find themselves competing for space in a scene resembling the Day of Judgement, according to some, or a barrel of herrings, according to others?

The short answer to these questions is that she succeeded simply through her personal qualities – charm, determination and courage. If it seems strange to identify courage as an ingredient, it has to be remembered how extraordinarily restricted Society was in the 1870s, when Mary started out. Gatherings were not just held for fun, they had an underlying structure and intent as serious as that of established religion. Most entertaining was done by political hostesses, who only invited guests who belonged to their husband's party. They might include aristocrats and senior clergy, but *not* people from the professional classes. As for those involved in trade... they could hardly even be mentioned. Straying from the confines of convention risked ostracisation – a fate worse than death. So there were very few hostesses who broke the rules, and they only dared to do so if they had the backing of a title and/or abundant wealth. It seems to have been one of these defiant Ladies who inspired Mary to follow her example. Her name was Frances Waldegrave.

Lady Waldegrave was the chatelaine of Strawberry Hill, the fairy-tale neo-gothic mansion in Twickenham built by Horace Walpole in the 18th century. She was born Frances Braham, daughter of a Jewish orphan from Whitechapel who had become a successful opera singer and impresario. John Braham was an international star, and could have been a wealthy man had he not insisted on ploughing his earnings back into the theatre, causing him to be bankrupt for most of his life. So Frances grew up in poverty, but her fortunes were transformed on a single evening which sparked a fortuitous chain of events.

One day John Braham was invited to Strawberry Hill by the 6th Earl Waldegrave, and he took his family along with him. Waldegrave's two dissolute sons immediately fell in love with the beautiful 17-year-old Frances. The older (illegitimate) son, John, proposed to her on the spot and she accepted. But within a year of their marriage John was dead, a victim to epilepsy. Now it was George's turn to marry Frances, and when his father died soon after, being a legitimate son he inherited Strawberry Hill and the title. Frances would now have been very comfortably off but for the fact that George was a serious gambler and drinker. Before long he was forced to sell the entire contents and furnishings of Strawberry Hill to pay off his debts. He set up a grand auction that lasted for nearly a month, and then proceeded to drink himself to death. At the age of only twenty five, twice-widowed, Frances inherited the entire Waldegrave estate, including the by now crumbling Strawberry Hill.

Next she very sensibly married a wealthy widower of sixty-one, which enabled her to restore the house to its former magnificence. It is hardly surprising that after sixteen years (of happy marriage, it has to be said) she was widowed yet again. Two days after the customary year of mourning elapsed, she married an Irish Liberal politician, Chichester Fortescue. She spent the rest of her days supporting his career, and by the 1860s she was the leading Liberal party hostess of the day.

This was when Mary got to know her. Her aunt Louisa would often take her to spend the weekend at Strawberry Hill, for Frances liked to have young people around her. Far from restricting her guest list to members of her husband's party, Frances scandalised her more exclusive friends by embracing members of the opposition, Irish nationalists, and even people from the artistic community. When eyebrows were raised at her unconventional visitors she would joke: 'I am sure everyone will say that they are some of my vulgar relatives.' With grudging admiration Queen Victoria noted in her diary: 'Ly Waldegrave is certainly a very clever woman. Mr Fortescue is her 4th Husband!' When Fortescue was appointed Chief Secretary for Ireland they moved to Dublin for a while. One night at the theatre some wag called out to Frances, 'And which of your four husbands does your Ladyship like the best?' Without missing a beat she responded, 'Why the Irishman of course', bringing the house down, and establishing herself as de facto queen of Dublin.

There were plenty of people who, even while enjoying her hospitality, disliked and despised Lady Waldegrave: she was not only an upstart but a 'Jewess' to boot. Mary however saw in her a kindred spirit. Frances was a devoted wife, a ready wit, and a great lover of romantic comedies and am-drams – all attributes that Mary shared. In her memoir Mary writes of Frances: 'She had the secret of success, which was a thorough enjoyment of her life and occupations.' Years later E.F. Benson, author of the *Mapp and Lucia* novels, would describe Mary in very similar terms:

Keen and tremendously alive, she had to a most exceptional degree that quality of a hostess without which all other gifts are worth nothing, namely that she immensely enjoyed her own parties.

After arriving in London Mary had quickly discovered that people of rank, i.e. those who don't need to work for a living, do not necessarily make for the most interesting company. In the 1870s there was a burgeoning middle class knocking on the doors of Society, but it required a brave hostess to let them in. Even doctors were not considered respectable enough to be admitted, while the theatre was regarded as a positive pit of depravity. When Mary started throwing her doors wide, following Frances Waldegrave's example, she had none of her advantages. Frances had plenty of money, and a title (she never allowed her subsequent marriages to deprive her of that). Mary's first husband was merely a failed Conservative politician, and they lived in comparatively straitened circumstances in a terraced house in Wimpole Street.

Nevertheless her gatherings were soon attracting attention from such dedicated socialites as Oscar Wilde, who gushes in a letter to her that 'the only place in London worth going to is your brilliant salon'. She widened her net early on. Plenty of Tories, friends of her husband, came to the house, where they would feel put out by finding members of the opposition also in attendance. Randolph Churchill in particular systematically ignored one such guest on many occasions, Mary each time going through 'the same little farce of introducing them to each other, Lord Randolph saying to him in a very innocent, irritating manner: "Ah! Yes, I believe I do recollect you at Eton!"'

This was mild compared to some of the altercations that would take place under her roof later on, but Mary had the ability to pour oil on the roughest water, and to get people who would never normally give each other the time of day chatting like old friends. 'She had an amount of tact, quickness, knowledge, and self sacrifice which few possess', said one contemporary, while the *Westminster Gazette* praised her for bringing 'social tact up to the point of high art'. Potentially awkward situations were handled with humour, such as the occasion (a particular favourite of mine) when, just before introducing a man to the woman he would sit next to at dinner, she murmured in his ear: 'Don't allude to railway accidents. Her aunt was cut to ribbons on the Underground.'

This is not to say that she didn't at first find it stressful mixing guests with opposing views. Since she was generally prone to understatement, it's unlikely that she is exaggerating when she uses words like 'audacious' to describe her early experiments in social diversity. She talks of feeling 'perilously near catastrophe' watching a High Church prelate conversing with an outspoken agnostic or socialist, and the 'terrible enjoyment of those Sunday afternoons'. (Because the weekend had not yet been invented, most visiting took place between three and seven o'clock on a Sunday.) By eight o'clock she would be exhausted, and glad to sit down to a quiet supper with her husband. George W. Smalley, American correspondent of the *Times*, wrote this accolade to her bravery:

> Lady Randolph Churchill once gave…what she called a dinner of deadly enemies. It was thought a hazardous experiment. What Lady Randolph did for that one evening Mrs Jeune did night after night and year after year… Mrs Jeune cast diplomacy to the winds. The one gift which stood to her in the place of all others was courage.

She soon became bolder. Her second marriage, to Francis Jeune, brought her into contact with various members of the legal profession, but as she tactfully remarks, she couldn't help feeling that it would be 'more agreeable' to host a more varied crowd. Soon establishment figures were mixing not only with scientists and doctors, but also bohemians: artists, actors, and writers – of both sexes. Mary found that visitors were not discouraged by the thought of meeting someone from a different walk of life – on the contrary, it was a great draw.

By the 1890s Mary was famous for the unique diversity of her social circle. An anecdote circulated, which told of an unhappy explorer who had found himself captured by cannibals, tied up and put in a pot ready for roasting. At this point the chief of the village comes out and recognises the explorer. 'Why,' he says, 'we have met at Mary Jeune's – you must come and dine with me, and tell me all the London news.'

In the twentieth century Mary became Lady St Helier, and to some extent a caricature of herself. Somerset Maugham recounts overhearing a conversation about someone suspected of a 'particularly callous' murder. A man was asking his friend if he knew the accused – the friend replied, 'No, but if he isn't hanged I shall certainly meet him at Lady St Helier's next week.'

This exotic reputation tends to distract from the qualities that made Mary so popular in the first place. If you were lucky enough to get one of those coveted invitations to her house, you would be welcomed by a surprisingly small woman with dark, piercing eyes that you might have found unsettling if she hadn't been so genuinely warm and interested in you, no matter who you were. And if there were detractors who wrote Mary off as a mere lion-hunter, there were many more disciples ready to leap to her defence. Years later E.F. Benson, recalling her heyday, wrote:

> Lady Jeune, afterwards Lady St Helier, a very catholic and distinguished hostess of the nineties and the succeeding decade, had nothing whatever in common with these ruthless Dianas... The lions in Lady St Helier's case eagerly sought her threshold and purred loudly on admittance... Every species of lion, barbarous or tame, flocked to her, cabinet ministers and channel-swimmers, poets and pugilists. Lady St Helier was more like a guest in her own house, having a most delightful evening.

Extravagance in Dress[2]

In which Mary's parents (and the spiritual domination of the Free Church of Scotland) leave her with a lifetime's aversion to extravagance of any kind

Mary Jeune began her life as Susan Mary Elizabeth Stewart Mackenzie, growing up in the Scottish highlands not far from Inverness. If as an adult she displayed singular qualities, I'm sure it's because she experienced a most unusual upbringing. It was peculiar for a degree of hardship that today would have social services knocking on the door. She and her three siblings subsisted on a diet of porridge for breakfast and porridge for tea, with the exception of Sundays when 'as a great treat' they had bread with butter and jam (but not both at the same time). Baths were in cold water, and sometimes in winter you had to break the ice on the surface before you could get in. They made do with a minimum of clothes:

> one warm frock for winter, with one change, and the same for summer. Such a luxury as a beautiful hat, or a pair of silk stockings and smart shoes was unknown, and we suffered from the painful consciousness of… a wardrobe out of which only ugly and useful garments ever appeared.

But Mary was not born into a family of impoverished crofters. Far from it. The Mackenzies owned vast swathes of the Highlands,

---

[2] Title of her 1893 article in the *National Review*, in which she let rip on the subject. Two years later she wrote 'The Ethics of Shopping', a piece liberally sprinkled with words like 'temptation' and 'seduction'.

their land at one stage stretching from Fortrose in the East to the Isle of Lewis in the West. Mary's grandmother, Mary Frederica Stewart Mackenzie, was chieftain of the Mackenzie clan and lived in Brahan[3] Castle near the town of Dingwall. Had it not been for a curse laid on the family in the seventeenth century, they would have been aristocrats – as it was the title had died out with her great-grandfather. (The prophecies of the Brahan Seer have been well documented elsewhere, but you can find the story of his curse on the family in the Appendix.)

Brahan Castle: 'a strange, ugly house', Mary thought it

In common with many other Scottish landowners, the Mackenzies struggled to make their estate profitable. There was a limit to how much rent you could demand of your tenants, and landlords had to look for other options to maintain their standard of living. One solution was to evict most of the tenants and turn the land over to sheep farming, a practice that many of them adopted; now infamous as the Highland Clearances, which left the landscape littered with deserted and ruined villages. Incidentally, the Brahan Seer apparently predicted this disastrous turn of events:

---

3   *Brahan* is pronounced Brawn, or if you're Scottish, *Brahn*

The day will come when the big sheep will put the plough up in the rafters ...
The big sheep will overrun the country till they meet the northern sea.

But the Mackenzies were not like other landowners. Mary's great-grandfather, Francis Humberston Mackenzie, had moral objections to ousting tenants who'd been there for generations. He refused to succumb to pressure from sheep farmers from the south, who were prepared to offer him triple the rent. He was, he said, 'anxious to keep together the people I looked on as heritably attached to my family.' His descendants continued to uphold this sense of *Noblesse Oblige* – you could perhaps say that it was in Mary's DNA. Of course it didn't help with their financial problems, but the poverty that the Mackenzies liked to complain of has to be seen in context. None of the males of the family ever thought of giving up gambling as a leisure pursuit, for instance, or downgrading their wine cellars. They preferred to pay their debts by selling off parcels of land, of which they had plenty.

Mary's father Keith was genuinely badly off, as he had no property of his own. When Mary was born he had recently retired from fighting in the Opium Wars. He married Mary's mother, Hannah Hope-Vere, and then spent his army pension on a protracted honeymoon – more than a year – in Bavaria, where Mary was born. When funds dried up he was forced to return to his mother's estate in the Highlands, a humiliating retreat which he always resented. While his mother, Mary Frederica, lived in relative style in the Castle, Keith and Hannah were dependent on her for a cramped and somewhat smelly cottage on the estate in which to house their family – it was, Keith said, 'in the midst of a kind of sewer or rather surrounded by sewers.'

Three more children followed Mary: Julia, Frank and Georgiana (always known as Moulie). Mary and Julia were tough enough, but Frank and Moulie often came close to death in illnesses which can't have been helped by the damp climate and the 'sewers'. Moulie remained fragile and was to die at eighteen, but Frank survived to pursue a long career in soldiery and marry an heiress in later life, giving him the means to live out his days in relative comfort in the Castle.

My grandmother had managed to hang on to some family letters dating from this time. Among them I found Mary's very first letter to her grandmother, and I reproduce it here because it is one of only three letters written by her that I have ever managed to track down. (I found two more in a shoe box at the Dorset County Museum – but we'll come to that later.)

Mary signs herself 'Little Wuz': a pet name presumably acknowledged even by her fearsome grandma

Along with this was a bundle of letters from Mary's parents to Mary Frederica. Apart from repeated concerns about sick children, Keith's letters to his mother consist of a litany of complaints about money: 'If you knew how poor I am and the straights [sic] I am in you would perhaps feel for me', he writes. Plainly she did not, having financial problems of her own: twice widowed, she was responsible for the upkeep of an enormous draughty castle and an unmarried daughter who was still at home. 'I wish to God we had the means to go to London & keep up our acquaintance,' wails Keith, yet when his mother tries to find work for him he writes to her that he cannot take it as he is getting old and deaf (he was not yet forty). And so he was stuck at Brahan, waiting for his inheritance to set him free.

Though cash flow may have been an issue, it was by no means the main cause of the spartan lifestyle imposed on the children. The real culprit was the Free Kirk of Scotland. Mary was born in 1845, just two years after the cataclysmic event known as the Great Disruption, probably the most divisive episode in Scottish history after the Jacobite rebellion.

In accordance with an Act passed in 1712, Church of Scotland ministers were appointed by local lairds. Discontent at this arrangement had been brewing for more than a century. Congregations felt, not unreasonably, that they should be the ones to choose who preached at them. All attempts at reforming the system were turned down by the government in London, who detected a whiff of revolution in the people's demands. And so in 1843 two hundred ministers and elders simply walked out of the General Assembly of the Church of Scotland, and announced their intention of starting a new church altogether. In all, a third of the established church ministers – 474 of them to be precise – abandoned their churches, manses, and stipends, and were followed by their flocks. The Free Kirk of Scotland was born, each member of the congregation supporting it to the tune of a penny a week. In the absence of church buildings, services were conducted in fields and on open hillsides.

The majority of landowners supported the established church, as was only natural in the face of a popular uprising. But Mary's family, the Stewart Mackenzies of Brahan Castle, joined forces with their tenants and took up the new religion, giving rise to an unusual sense of solidarity between the classes. The passions provoked by the Disruption ran extremely high – Mary remembers as a small child being made to cross the road in order to avoid a minister of the established Church who was coming the other way.

Mary's mother Hannah embraced the 'spiritual domination' of the church she'd married into with the deep fervour of a convert. Mary's account of how they spent the Sabbath day deserves reproducing in some detail:

> I think it was not so much the quality of the religious teaching as its quantity that tried one's fidelity. A Sunday which began at eleven by a two and a half hour's service in Gaelic, with an interval of one hour for dinner, and was continued in English until half past three or four, was trying enough. There was no ritual and there was no music… The rest of Sunday was occupied in studying and reading the Bible and voluminous tracts…the Shorter Catechism was a hard enough nut for anybody to crack, but the Longer Catechism, which was taught after the difficulties and mysteries of the Shorter Catechism had been mastered, was something quite indescribably terrible. Sunday was a day full of gloom and darkness.

She writes without rancour about the process of 'hardening and bracing' which included home education administered by her mother, a 'stern, inexorable tutor' who had the children learning quantities of Shakespeare, Pope, and Milton by heart. But their childhood was not unhappy. The children were often farmed out to tenants on the estate, presumably so that the parents could go and stay with neighbouring landowners miles away. Mary describes these episodes, where life was even more basic, as some of the happiest of her childhood. There the children could run wild and free in an untamed landscape. Lessons were halted, while the family they stayed with substituted the harsh doctrines of the Free Kirk with a thorough education in Gaelic superstitions and fairy tales.

It was only when I read the account of her childhood in her memoir that I realised that Mary and I had something important in common. As a child I spent every summer holiday at Brahan, like Mary running wild and embracing traditional superstitions. My grandmother moved there just before I was born. The estate should have been handed down through a different branch of the family, but when my grandmother's two male cousins were killed within 24 hours of each other in WW2, she inherited it. (To us this looked like further proof of the family curse.) By this time the Castle was riddled with dry rot. Even without the rot it was an ugly building, far too big for my grandparents, and would have been impossibly expensive to maintain.

Luckily my father was on the spot to combine his wartime training as a sapper with his pre-war training as an architect. He blew up the castle with gelignite, leaving a romantic ruin. He then converted the elegant Georgian stables into a sunny south-facing house from which my grandmother could look out at the remains of the castle.

The happiest days of my childhood were spent at Brahan, climbing about on the dangerously unstable ruin or playing in the mystical Dell, an arboretum planted by Mary's great-grandfather, Francis Humberston Mackenzie. By penetrating far enough into its depths, where the canopy of ancient trees overhead blocked out the sun, you would eventually detect in the shadows the spooky gleam of a marble angel. Surrounded by a fortress of rhododendrons, and the graves of many faithful family dogs, the angel stood guarding the final resting place of great-uncle Frank, Mary's brother.

The romantic ruin, captured by me with my Brownie box camera when I was 10

Mary's father Keith seems to have been perpetually disgruntled. He did not like being stuck at Brahan after the sociable life of Munich, and he often fell out with his younger sister Louisa, who lived in the castle with Mary Frederica. Their squabbles are recorded in Keith's plaintive letters to his mother, and give the impression that her replies inevitably took Louisa's side. Keith was no match for his mother.

Mary Frederica was a powerful woman who had lived life to the full. When her first husband was posted in India she had taken advantage of his position to roam the country with a team of bearers, hunting down artefacts and wild game. She travelled as far as the North-West frontier, and claimed to be the first woman to shoot a tiger, which was quite possibly true. As for the artefacts, she went to great lengths to smuggle them back to Brahan, where they occupied an upstairs boudoir whose exotic ambience – inlaid and japanned cabinets, camphorwood chests, rugs and weavings and a small stuffed leopard – was in stark contrast with the masculine demeanour of the Castle's main rooms, bristling as they did with antlers and armaments.

Walter Scott was a great admirer of Mary Frederica's 'wild and almost lawless spirit of adventure', and she was the model for his Ellen Douglas, Lady of the Lake. (In spite of Scott being a good friend of their grandmother's, Mary and her siblings were forbidden to read his works before they reached the age of sixteen.) So if we want to find a significant influence in Mary's early life, or some powerful genetic material, I suggest we need look no further than her grandmother.

Before the railway penetrated that far north, the Mackenzies were effectively cut off from the outside world. Newspapers took three days to arrive, and visitors were few and far between. The children hardly travelled further afield than Inverness, about seventeen miles away, but one winter when Mary and Julia were in their teens Hannah took them to Edinburgh for some polishing of their education – things like dancing and music which were then considered vital skills for young ladies.

Mary found the inhabitants of the capital to be 'nearly as narrow and bigoted as their northern brethren'. But it was there that she experienced the greatest event of her life so far – going to the theatre. This was an entertainment generally viewed as ungodly by the Scots, but luckily Hannah considered Shakespeare to be sufficiently educational to allow them to breach convention. She took the girls to a series of Charles Kean Shakespeare revivals in Edinburgh's only theatre. 'What a joy that was!' says Mary, with a rare excursion into exclamation marks. The theatre may have been old and dilapidated, and the audiences half-hearted, but for Mary it was a revelation which turned her into a devoted theatre-goer for the rest of her life.

Mary became closer to her grandmother for the few years before her death. Aunt Louisa finally got married and moved out of the castle, while Mary's family moved in to take care of Mary Frederica. When Mary was eighteen Mary Frederica died. This was the cue for a Great Highland Funeral: all business in the adjoining villages was suspended for the day and people came from all over the country, forming a five-mile-long procession to the family burial ground at Fortrose on the east coast, twenty miles away. The cortège, led by a wailing dirge of pipers, left Brahan Castle at eleven o'clock in the morning and arrived at Fortrose at half-past three in the afternoon, while all along the way the bells of the churches tolled the funeral knell.

This was not exactly what Mary Frederica had planned. In her will she had clearly stated that her funeral should be conducted in the plainest manner and only in the presence of her nearest relations. 'If I shall die at Brahan', she wrote, 'my body shall be conveyed by sea to London, whence I desire it may be sent by railway to Southampton and wherever I may die that it may be placed in the Colonnade under the Church of All Saints in that town, where I have purchased a niche adjoining that of my late husband.' Whether that niche is still vacant, awaiting her corpse, I do not know. Mary Frederica's passing at last allowed Keith Stewart Mackenzie to leave 'this most beastly stupid country' and move to London with his family. Brahan Castle was rented out, and he never went back.

Mary never shook off the habit of frugality, nor the principle of *noblesse oblige*. She remained thrifty to an absurd degree, hating to spend money on a cab (which she could well afford) when there was the option of a penny omnibus. In later life she took to boasting about her childhood diet consisting mainly of porridge, and the fact that she never tasted chocolate until she was fifteen. In print she decried 'the craze among women to overdress themselves and multiply their gowns.' She summed it up quite simply: 'English women spend too much money on their dress and have too many clothes'.

London in the Sixties

In which Mary has her education broadened by two uncompromising women

Moving to London in 1863 must have been very exciting for young Mary. Previously she'd never been further south than Edinburgh, by comparison a grim, dour capital . Now free of the restraining hand of her mother, Mary was able to sample the grubby underbelly of the metropolis, and to meet a great variety of interesting people.

Mary's mother, who Keith condemned as a 'terrible stay-at-home old lady', was in fact quite unwell, and was to die within five years of the move. It seems that Keith used Mary as a stand-in when Hannah was unwilling, or unable, to join him. In this way she enjoyed a far more stimulating social life than she would have done otherwise, for, as she frequently likes to inform us, 'girls were hardly ever asked out to dinner'.

She was proud to have sat between Charles Dickens and Edward Bulwer Lytton at one dinner. Dickens' health was failing and he wasn't enjoying the party, but Mary says that Lytton was 'exceedingly nice' to her. I'm sure he was delighted to find an attractive young woman sitting next to him. Lytton is chiefly remembered now for coining the most clichéd opening words of a novel ('It was a dark and stormy night…'), and Mary was probably unaware that this was a man who had had his wife locked away in a mental asylum when she took to challenging him in front of his friends. (She was released in response to public outcry, and got her own back by outing him in a memoir called *A Blighted Life*).

Dinner parties were all very well, but what Mary craved, after eighteen years in the wholesome environment of the Scottish highlands, was a taste of forbidden fruit. And racy Aunt Loo was just the person to facilitate this. Louisa Stewart Mackenzie, by now Lady Ashburton, was an extremely spirited woman, described by a contemporary as 'generous, violent, rash and impulsive'. During her years at Brahan Castle, in between time spent teaching at the school in Dingwall, she had conducted a series of romantic relationships by post, mostly with other women. Florence Nightingale, who was one of them, later insisted that Louisa destroy their correspondence. Mary Frederica must have felt frustrated at Loo's refusal to marry for so long, even though she had Edwin Landseer as a suitor – but then he was wedded to the bottle.

Louisa was thirty-one by the time she married Lord Ashburton, a wealthy neighbour twenty-eight years her senior. Unsurprisingly, she was widowed after only six years, but not before producing a child, Mary Florence, named after Nightingale but generally known as Maysie. An aunt had once told Loo that 'there is a thirst in your soul or your *heart*, that nothing earthly will ever satisfy', and this certainly seems to have been the case. After Ashburton's death Louisa managed to conduct affairs concurrently with the poet Robert Browning and the American sculptor Harriet Hosmer, whom she had met in Rome. Hatty Hosmer, a small rotund woman who liked to sport a jacket and cravat, immediately fell under Loo's spell and would remain there for many years, styling herself 'hubby' and Loo her '*sposa*'.

The relationship with Browning was less successful. His heart still lay in Florence where Elizabeth was buried, and although Loo spread the word that he had proposed to her, and that she had refused, in reality it was the other way round. He began to avoid her. When he did accidentally bump into her he minded her, he said, 'no more than any other black beetle – so long as it dont crawl up my sleeve.' His antipathy to Louisa did not stop him from becoming a good friend of Mary's, in spite of her often telling him that she 'had never been able to read a line of his poetry'.

When Mary moved to London, Lord Ashburton was recently deceased and Louisa was free to enjoy the leisured life of a woman who now owned five properties, in Scotland, Devon, Cornwall, Hampshire, and London. She was happy to grant Mary's wish to visit Cremorne Gardens, a pleasure park of louche repute down by the Thames. It consisted of twelve acres of gardens with mature trees, fountains and a lake, stretching from Battersea Bridge to the King's Road.

During the day it was respectable enough, full of families who for a one shilling entrance fee could enjoy such delights as a marionette theatre, a maze, a hermit's cave and a fairy grotto. Entertainments included equestrian displays, balloon ascents, and death-defying feats: the 'Female Blondin' who crossed the river from Battersea to Cremorne on a tightrope; Madame Poitevin, who was hoisted skywards by balloon, seated on a live heifer and representing Europa; the 'Italian Salamander', a man who entered a burning furnace with apparent unconcern; and the Great Valerio, who for three months in 1863 performed on a wire rope slung between two tall trees. Unfortunately not all these acts defied death successfully, for one night in June the Great Valerio's rope broke. He fell 60ft to the ground and fractured his skull, dying in agony in the Chelsea Hospital the following morning.

If Mary had been hoping to witness one of these spectacles for which Cremorne was famed she may have been disappointed, as dangerous acrobatics were now banned from the gardens. But there was still the lure of burlesque and magic, magnificent firework displays, supper rooms and the Crystal Pagoda. The pagoda was a fabulous attraction, its ironwork encrusted with emerald and garnet, and the whole thing festooned with hundreds of tiny gaslights whose effect was multiplied by plate glass mirrors. Bands played from an upper floor, lit by seventeen gas chandeliers, while dancing platforms encircled the pagoda at ground level.

As it grew dark and the families departed, the gardens filled up with those seeking less salubrious pleasures. Toffs spilled out of

The Crystal Pagoda in Cremorne gardens

their carriages, prostitutes lurked in the shadows, drunken young blades arrived from the races, and sometimes fights broke out. The gardens were now 'a nursery for every kind of vice', according to the local Baptist minister. While it attracted a fashionable crowd of posers, notably James Abbott McNeill Whistler (who would later become one of Mary's favourite dinner guests) it certainly was not to the liking of most local residents. Thomas Carlyle, who lived just along the Embankment on Cheyne Walk, complained bitterly of 'Cremorne and its nauseous uproar'. A series of petitions were mounted against the licensee on grounds of the 'immorality' which spilled out into the surrounding streets, and in 1877 the Gardens were closed for ever and housing built on the site. A tiny park today remains at the end of Lots Road, with only the imposing wrought-iron gates and a statue of Whistler giving a clue to Cremorne's former glory.

Another place that was quite unsuitable for young ladies was Evans' Supper Rooms in Covent Garden, where Mary's father took her more than once. A cavernous dining hall with a stage at one end provided food and entertainment for an entirely male clientele who chatted and smoked into the small hours. They could sing along with lewd songs, or listen to madrigals sung by choirs of beautiful boys. Women had very recently been admitted, but only on condition that they give their names and addresses – a precaution against prostitution – and that they sit in an upper gallery behind a grille, rather like in the House of Commons (where Mary was also often taken). But she found this late-night event thrilling enough to overlook the discomfort of her hot, stuffy 'prison' – besides, the cheap supper of 'grilled bones' (chops) and toasted cheese she thought a great treat.

These adventures seem to have satisfied Mary's appetite for low-life entertainments, for she makes no further mention of them. At the more conventional level there was of course the mandatory round of balls and country weekends where you were supposed to find a suitable husband, but Mary was lucky. Although it is rumoured that she had a proposal from a duke, she does not seem to have been put under undue pressure to marry, unlike many other young women whose impecunious families were desperate to have them off their hands.

This had been the fate of a woman who lived in Chesterfield Street, just around the corner from the Stewart Mackenzies, and who Mary visited 'constantly' – which is odd, as although Mrs Norton often gave dinners for eight or ten people, you would not find another woman there – her guests were all men. Now nearly sixty, Caroline Norton was a witty, flirtatious woman who insisted on being the star of her own dinner party – indeed woe betide her guests if they dared to interrupt her. Mrs Norton had a very bad temper, and given her history it was hardly surprising.

She was born Caroline Sheridan in 1808, a granddaughter of Richard Brinsley Sheridan, author of *The School for Scandal*. Like many well-connected families of the time the Sheridans had no money, and so they married Caroline off at nineteen to an unsuccessful barrister by the name of George Norton, a man she barely knew and who turned out to be a violent drunk. After ten years of physical abuse she left him, whereupon he confiscated her jewellery, her children, and the not inconsiderable income from her writing – she was the author of several popular songs as well as books of prose and poetry. Not content with that, he took her to court for 'criminal conversation' (a Victorian euphemism for adultery) with Lord Melbourne, the then Home Secretary. This was particularly sly, as he had encouraged Caroline's friendship with Melbourne in the hopes of getting work for himself.

When it became clear that Norton had bribed the witnesses, the case was thrown out. This had the unfortunate result that Caroline was chained to Norton for life, as women could not initiate divorce. Meanwhile the press had a field day with reporting all the seamy details of the case. The scandalous reportage in such vulgar rags as *Crim Con Gazette* destroyed Caroline's reputation for ever, and for the next six years Norton denied her access to her three sons.

So Caroline did what she knew best how – she took up her pen and started to pour out impassioned writings, with the aim of changing the law. She started with the pithily-titled *Observations on the Natural Claims of a Mother to the Custody of her Children As Affected by the Common Law Rights of the Father*. Relentless campaigning eventually got results. In 1839 the Custody of Infants Act was passed, allowing women *some* rights over their own children for the first time. Unfortunately the law did not apply to Scotland, where Caroline's husband kept the boys out of her reach. It was only the death of their youngest son that eventually weakened his appetite for revenge. Caroline continued to campaign for the next twenty years, and in 1857 she wrote a 30,000-word letter to Queen Victoria detailing the inequalities of the law regarding married women. That year the Matrimonial Causes Act was passed, giving women the right to start divorce proceedings.

Although Caroline achieved so much for married women's rights she was no feminist, and had few women friends. She was quite happy to admit that she 'never pretended to the wild and ridiculous doctrine of equality'. At the dinner parties which Mary attended, Caroline expected 'a large amount of attention and deference from her guests'. Even so there were a couple of men who tried to stand up to her, causing discussions to become 'very animated'. Among them was Richard Monckton Milnes, the father of Florence Henniker (who would later become the object of much attention from Thomas Hardy). Monckton Milnes was famed for his piety, less well-known for his peerless collection of erotic literature. There was also a Mr Charles Villiers, who 'had a very sarcastic and sharp tongue [and] occasionally interpolated remarks which aroused Mrs Norton's anger.' Meanwhile Mary sat there quietly, observing.

Even now, Caroline Norton's sufferings were not over. She had quite recently watched her eldest son dying of tuberculosis, while the younger one was a physical and mental wreck, living on the isle of Capri and demanding constant financial support. She was still able to earn enough money by writing to support him and his daughter Carlotta, who was now living with her at Chesterfield Street, because her father's behaviour was at best erratic, at worst abusive.

Mary noticed that Caroline had great difficulty keeping domestic staff, and expected her granddaughter to do menial tasks around the house. This didn't go down well with the girl who was in her early teens, and who 'in addition to her father's wild temperament, had inherited the passionate nature of her Italian mother'. More sparks flew.

Why Mary was so often in attendance at those men-only dinners is something of a mystery. Mary thinks it was because she was only a girl, and therefore no rival to the still-beautiful Mrs Norton, but that seems a little naive. Perhaps it was because Mary knew many of the songs that Caroline had written, and was happy to sing them for her, even if she privately thought them sentimental and 'twaddly'.

Or could it have been to do with a link to the Stewart Mackenzie family that Mary probably knew nothing about? For Aunt Louisa, in the days when she was still living at Brahan, had for many years been desperately in love with a man called William Stirling. But he never returned her feelings because *he* loved the very-much married Caroline Norton. At the time Loo had written: 'I often think I will wait till I am old and he is old and then see what happens, she can't always last so beautiful…' But in the end, it was Caroline who in old age married William Stirling. She was sixty-nine when George Norton's death finally set her free, and she enjoyed three happy months of life with William before peritonitis tragically put an end to it.

Mrs Norton's youthful beauty has been preserved forever as the Spirit of Justice, the central figure of a fresco in the House of Lords, and thanks to a recent biography by Antonia Fraser, *The Case of the Married Woman,* she has finally had a blue plaque installed on her house at no. 3 Chesterfield Street. In Mary's memoir Caroline appears in the index only as 'Mr Norton', suggesting that despite fifty odd years of campaigning, attitudes had hardly changed since she first defined the married woman thus: 'She does not exist – her husband exists.'

The Stanleys of Alderley

In which Mary marries into a family famed for its bad behaviour as much as for its brilliance

Mary must have had some idea of what she was taking on when she decided to marry Johnny Stanley, my great-great-grandfather. The Mackenzies and the Stanleys had been on friendly terms for at least two generations, and the Stanley family were notorious for their loud and public disagreements. Johnny's father Edward was famed for making spiteful remarks, so much so that he was known as Ben, after Sheridan's anti-hero Sir Benjamin Backbite in *School for Scandal*. If Johnny had inherited his father's malicious sense of humour, it was not going to put Mary off. More than once in her memoir she expresses admiration for people she knew during her early days in

John Constantine Stanley, with dog

London who 'inspired terror' because of their sharp tongues. Mary was not daunted – on the contrary she seems to have actively sought their company.

Johnny's parents, Lord Edward and Lady Henrietta Stanley, were the progenitors of a large family of intellectual titans, whose views on religion and politics differed to an extreme degree. Each and every one of them stuck to the firm conviction that they were right, even if this resulted in them falling out irreparably with a child or sibling – which it often did. In fact many of their actions were apparently motivated solely by the desire to annoy other members of the family. Their supreme indifference to what the rest of the world might think of them was a trait that Mary seemed to find particularly attractive. Nowadays they tend to be regarded as bonkers aristocrats who created storms because they couldn't bear to be bored.

In the twentieth century Henrietta and Edward Stanley's great-great-granddaughters, the Mitford sisters, followed the family tradition of conducting their disagreements in public by espousing political views of every shade from communism through to nazism, and scandalising the general public who read all about their escapades in the newspapers. Luckily for this story Nancy, the oldest sister, devoted herself to collecting and editing the many letters that passed between three generations of Stanleys. Without this I would have known very little about my great-great-grandfather (which in some ways might have been a blessing).

In the introduction to her book *The Stanleys of Alderley* Nancy professes a particular fondness for Johnny, a delicate child but the naughtiest by far. His father Edward seems to have spent a lot of time escaping from the chaos at home, leaving Henrietta to deal with their turbulent brood. Henrietta's letters to Edward sometimes verge on desperation:

> It is impossible I think to find a much naughtier boy than Johnny, his mind is filled with filthiness and evil speaking. He swears, says every improper thing he can think of to his sisters.

He continually flouted the house rules by bringing the dogs into his bedroom, he chased the housemaids with a spear, and was expelled from Harrow at fourteen for foul language and rude behaviour, such as jumping over the headmaster's table at dinner and insulting the tradespeople. Another time Henrietta writes:

> Johnny looks very pale, is very thin, & is much more selfish and naughty than I ever saw him before. Speaks to Lyulph [a brother] & indeed to all the little ones as if they were dogs – it makes one more unhappy than even his health.

And again: 'Johnny *very* naughty, disagreeable and pettish, he is now in punishment for throwing things at Eliza's head.' In spite of all this bad behaviour Johnny was a favourite not only of Nancy Mitford's, but also of his parents. 'Poor dear Johnny,' wrote his father, 'with all his little wildnesses he will turn out, I believe, the best of all.' These 'little wildnesses' caused a good deal of domestic mayhem. Bertrand Russell (another member of the tribe) relates an occasion when Johnny's sister Blanche first brought her new husband back to stay at the family home. When asked in the morning if he had slept well, Lord Airlie complained that his bed had been made 'apple pie'. (For those too young to remember, the apple pie bed was a popular trick to play before the advent of the duvet: you folded the bottom sheet up and over the blankets, so that when your victim got into bed their legs hit a barrier half way down.) 'Consternation ensued', says Russell, and all the servants were brought in to be interrogated. Eventually it was Henry, the firstborn, who owned up to the deed. This was a great surprise to everyone, as Henry was the most sedate member of the family, and quite old enough to know better. His father, furious, asked him why on earth he had done such a thing. 'I had to' he said, 'because Johnny stood over me with a pistol and said he would shoot me if I didn't.'

The current generation may find Johnny's outrageous behaviour less amusing than Nancy Mitford did, but one has to admire his refusal to allow constant illness to cramp his style. At the age of sixteen he went off to fight in Crimea, apparently filled with an intense longing to kill a Russian. But in the searing heat of Balaclava he went down with dysentery, and had to be sent home after only a month without fulfilling his ambition. His Commander General Brownrigg wrote:

> He is a very nice boy and we are all very fond of him. He ought not to have been sent out at sixteen to rough it here as he is obliged to do. He has not stamina for it... He is not a good patient, poor little fellow, he is altered so as to have lost all his good looks & resembles a sick girl of 11 or 12.

Johnny's next venture was to India at the time of the 1857 Sepoy Rebellion, where his aim was to 'shoot niggers in action' – or at the very least to stick a pig, according to his letters home. Lady Stanley was a staunch Whig with liberal views, and over the course of their correspondence she frequently objects to his use of the N-word. She even sought the support of Bishop Cotton of Calcutta, whose opinion was that 'Hindoos are no more niggers than Johnny himself.'

Johnny really didn't like India. What he did like was provoking his mother, and describing acts of violence in grisly detail. His post was that of ADC to Lord Canning, Governor General of India, where he was the youngest member of staff. Much of his work seems to have consisted of entertaining the ladies, whom he accompanied to the hills in the hot season, his delicate health being taken into account. Lady Canning was a botanist and an accomplished artist (a substantial collection of her sketches and watercolours can be seen in the V&A Museum). Johnny adored her and she was clearly fond of him, always referring to him as 'little Johnny Stanley'. She writes:

> He is like a merry page, so civil & useful, but he requires care, his chest is weak... everywhere everyone is ready to spoil him, he is so nice & amusing... Johnny's spirits never flag as you may easily

believe & he enlivens our little party more than I can say... I never saw such an affectionate creature.

Her cousin Mrs Stuart's opinion of him was less enthusiastic:

We are usually a silent set easily daunted except the dauntless boy J. Stanley of whom we get far more than is good for himself, though Char [Lady Canning] spoils him at one time, scolds him at another & thinks she keeps him in order.

Johnny didn't like Mrs Stuart much either:

She is absurdly jealous when I show my preference for Lady Canning – of course I like walking with her, she walks like a goat while Mrs S. puffs and blows and requires lifting over stones 1 ft high.

Johnny was a keen photographer and the Met Museum in New York holds a collection of pictures he took in India, many of Lady Canning of course, and some which include Mrs Stuart. If I had permission I would reproduce one here...

Five years in India did nothing to improve Johnny's opinion of it, and as his term of service drew to an end he wrote to his mother asking her to tell Lady Canning how he had worshipped her –

for I cannot well say so to her face... Here I am in this horrid steaming place, very wretched, do what I will to amuse myself without Lady Canning. Campbell Beale and Hills [fellow soldiers] are no friends of mine, the two latter are snobs... they always want to give their nasty hot arms to ladies on every occasion, their idea of a *lady* being a helpless fool or cripple.

Johnny was fond of using the word 'snob' to describe people he didn't like, perhaps unaware that it might equally be applied to himself. Wretched he may have been without Lady Canning, but he was not going to miss her husband when he came home.

> Lord C will not break his heart, no more shall I, when we say goodbye, yet I have served him honestly & to the best of my powers although I have never taken to him. I wish he had a firmer mouth, it does so spoil his face.

Johnny clearly had oodles of charm, especially with the ladies, and Mary was nothing if not susceptible to charm. By the time she married Johnny he was 34, and had perhaps calmed down to some extent. We know nothing of their courtship. Johnny wrote regularly to his mother, but no mention of Mary appears in Nancy Mitford's book. Unfortunately, after it was published Nancy lost all the original correspondence, so any reference to Mary is lost forever. However I did find one in a letter from Lady Henrietta to her daughter Kate, in Bertrand Russell's *Amberley Papers*. She sounds very pleased:

> We are all in great excitement – Johnny is engaged to be married to Miss Mackenzie – he has known and cared for her for three years. She is a very loveable person clever accomplished & very sensible in all she says… I am so very happy that at last one is married… I think Mary so very nice – she is very liberal! only think & likes reading and sensible things. I am sure you will like her – at least I hope so…'

During the first years of her marriage, before any babies arrived, Mary spent a lot of time in Stanley company. A regular event was Sunday lunch at her mother-in-law's house in Dover Street, Mayfair, where the strident discourse either helped Mary to sharpen up her debating skills, or forced her to remain silent. 'The vehemence with which every person upheld his own, the perfect frankness with which each dissented from the others, filled me with speechless admiration,' she says.

Presiding over the cacophony was Lady Henrietta, a formidable matriarch, High Church liberal and champion of women's education, but staunchly opposed to Home Rule and women's suffrage. Her husband Edward had died a couple of years before Mary and Johnny married, at which, according to Nancy Mitford, Henrietta instantly metamorphosed from a gentle, suppliant spouse with golden curls into a 'solid matron with beady eye and hooky nose... the terror of all who came into contact with her'.

Lady Henrietta Stanley

Henrietta's first act after Edward died was to help found Girton, Britain's first women's college, along with Barbara Bodichon and Emily Davies. According to Nancy Mitford she 'failed to apply her principles to her own daughters, who were brought up without any knowledge of science or the classics and could not even spell or punctuate in their native language.' This is almost certainly an exaggeration. All the girls were clever and well-informed, and as disputatious as their brothers.

At Girton Lady Stanley fitted up a 'charming laboratory' for the Professor of Mathematics and Natural Science, Miss Herschel, who was a young woman in her twenties. Henrietta was very annoyed when she found that Miss Herschel was engaged to be married. 'It is no use having professors so young and so pretty,' she complained. She maintained a lifelong influence on Girton, refusing to allow college funds to be spent on a chapel. Just before she died she convened a meeting of governors at her house, where she carried on issuing orders from her deathbed. Building on the chapel started as soon as she was in her grave.

Henrietta produced twelve children over a period of eighteen years, nine of whom survived to adulthood. The oldest of these was Henry, who would not attend the Dover Street lunches because by this time he had fallen out completely with the rest of the family. As soon as Edward died Henry had inherited his title, and the estate at Nether Alderley in Cheshire. From a very young age he had been drawn to the East – at the age of twelve he asked his parents for an Arabic grammar, and later he converted to Islam, trying to keep this a secret from his family whom he knew would disapprove. Eventually his cover was blown by headlines in the popular press trumpeting THE ENGLISH MAHOMEDAN. In a letter to Henrietta, his father went berserk.

> There is a paragraph in the Morning Post about that wretched fool Henry, saying he was at Penang living entirely with Mahometans & dressed in their dress. He was, it said, living with a certain Sheikh Salim Bangadie, speaking Arabic perfectly & avoiding the society of Europeans. Is he mad or what is he?
>
> What has Henry to do with Arabs at Penang, they are an inferior & degraded class of people & it is disgraceful his associating with them.

What Edward never knew was that Henry had also got married secretly, to a Spanish lady called Fabia, in three or four separate ceremonies: Islamic ones in Algeria and Turkey, in a registry office in Britain, and again in a Catholic church to please Fabia. The family only discovered this after their father's death – Henry revealed the fact to his mother as her train was pulling out of the station after the funeral. By then he had been married for seven years and it was far too late for anyone to do anything about it. Luckily for the family, it turned out that Fabia had a previous husband in Spain, still alive, so all the weddings were bigamous. She never had any children which saved a lot of complications later, when Henry died, and the estate could pass smoothly to his brother Lyulph.

Although Henry carries the distinction of being Britain's first Muslim peer, his family were not in the slightest impressed by him. He was quite deaf, which made him difficult to communicate with at the best of times, and Bertrand Russell said that he was the greatest bore he ever knew. But when in 1903 Henry's death was announced to the Indian National Congress, the 1,800-strong assembly rose to its feet as a mark of respect, for he had been a stern critic of British imperialism. He was buried in a small plantation on the Alderley estate, facing Mecca, with prayers led by the Imam from the Turkish Embassy in London.

Next in line after Henry came Alice, who married the eccentric ethnographer Augustus Lane Fox in 1853. In 1880 Augustus inherited the Rushmore estate and the name Pitt Rivers, four years later founding the Oxford museum of that name. The current curators believe that Augustus acquired his passion for collecting exotic artefacts from the Stanleys, who themselves owned an impressive collection of ethnographic items, including souvenirs of India that Johnny had brought back with him. Alice, like her mother, was a great breeder, producing nine children in ten years. She had a reputation for extreme stinginess, and had been witnessed returning uneaten food from a guest's plate to the serving dish. She was pro-suffrage, and the least favourite child of Henrietta, who was shameless about showing her preferences, or lack of them. On the other hand she got on well with Henry, and was the first sibling to accept Fabia – who the rest of the family dismissed as 'mad and impossible'.

After Alice came Blanche, who was inclined to be superstitious, a red flag to her rationalist mother who used to lay thirteen places at the table just to annoy her. Blanche's granddaughter Clementine was to end up married to Winston Churchill, and her great-granddaughters were the Mitford sisters. It was Blanche's husband who had been the recipient of the apple-pie bed, and Blanche who was closest to Johnny.

Next in line was Maude, who was low church, didn't marry, and ran girls' clubs in Soho. She was a kind person, and the daughter that Mary would spend most time with, having a shared interest in good causes. After Maude came Johnny, the only Conservative in this staunchly Whig, progressive family. This meant that at the Dover Street lunches Mary had the unenviable task of defending his views to the rest of them.

Then there was Lyulph, who was Henrietta's favourite. He was a brilliant wit, an atheist, and a republican, with views too radical for success in public life, but that hardly mattered because when Henry died he inherited the title. Lyulph was not welcome on the Alderley estate while Henry was alive – on one occasion he had him chased off by the gamekeeper.

Algernon, said by some to be the nicest, was plump and genial. He had himself been in love with Mary, but having failed to marry her he turned to the Cloth. He should have been the vicar for the parish of Alderley, but as Henry wouldn't allow him onto the estate he took his revenge by converting to Catholicism, and ended his life rather comfortably as a bishop in Rome.

The most radical of all the Stanley offspring was Kate: a champion of birth control, free love and women's suffrage. When she died of diphtheria in 1875, aged thirty two, her husband Lord Amberley lost the will to live. He died soon after, leaving their two sons, Frank and Bertrand Russell, as orphans. When Bertrand reached the age of seven he would appear at Dover Street, anxious to impress his grandmother. The budding mathematician proudly told Lady Henrietta that he had grown 2½ inches in the last seven months, and that at that rate he would grow four-and-two-sevenths inches in a year. To which Henrietta responded: 'Don't you know that you should never talk about any fractions except halves and quarters? It is pedantic!' To a guest she said: 'I have no intelligent grandchildren.'

The youngest sibling, Rosalind, was married to an artist, later an Earl, George Howard. They were in with the Pre-Raphaelite set, and she had several portraits of herself painted by Dante Gabriel

Rossetti. Like her mother and Alice, she was a great bearer of babies, producing twelve children at two-year intervals. Her religious position was agnostic, her politics were pro Home Rule for Ireland. She employed an Irish tutor, who at Lady Stanley's table was brave enough to express surprise that a woman of her formidable intelligence could not see the case for Home Rule. According to Bertand Russell, Henrietta 'put her starers to her eyes, looked at him for some time, and then said: "Mr Jones, I hate a fool".' Rosalind was an ardent temperance campaigner. She emptied her husband's entire wine cellar into the lake and closed down the public houses on her estates, just as Henry had done at Alderley in accordance with his Islamic principles. In later life she became as tyrannical as her mother, and fell out with most of her children.

There was a ten-year gap between Johnny and Henry. Their relationship was alternately fond and hostile. Russell recounts Johnny winding up his brother by buying a little Buddha and dedicating the breakfast to it. When Henry eyed up the tempting spread and asked his brother whether he'd dedicated *everything* to Buddha, Johnny said: 'All but the ham dear boy'. But it was to Johnny that he confided, in a sad letter from Penang, 'you know I have always been a Mussulman at heart.'

Their relationship must have soured subsequently. Johnny, always plagued by ill health, was only 40 when he died. Mary wanted to install a memorial to him in the church at Alderley, but Henry refused to let her. Full of the righteous indignation for which the Stanleys were famed, he declared that Johnny was 'a bad man, and no memorial to him should defile the sacred precincts.' This was harsh, considering that the church of St Mary at Alderley is nothing if not a shrine to the Stanley family. One side of the chancel is taken up by a stone sarcophagus with a bronze plaque on its side, portraying Henrietta and her family, while a life-sized effigy of Edward lies on top. The plaque depicts Henrietta enthroned, with the nine children who made it to adulthood on either side, and the three babies who didn't on her lap. Memorials to other family

The Stanley Sarcophagus in St Mary's Church Nether Alderley

members litter the church and graveyard, the most grandiose being an enormous neo-Jacobean mausoleum built by Lyulph. It dwarfs the churchyard and blocks the view of meadows beyond, and seems quite unnecessarily huge, given that the only remains it houses are the ashes of Lyulph and his wife. The parish council uses it for storage.

Above the nave to one side is the Stanley family 'pew' – actually an upstairs room big enough to accommodate the entire family, and providing a good vantage point from which the Earl could look down on his tenants. You enter it from the outside, via a set of stone steps. Access to the family vault is also outside, under one of the enormous flags that pave the churchyard. This is where Johnny was buried, and nearly twenty years later his mother Henrietta. After that the family somehow lost track of the entrance for more than a century, and it was only when work was being done on the church in 2007 that an architect found the steps leading down to the crypt. It contains just six coffins: those of Johnny, his parents, his grandparents, and a tiny one belonging to his uncle Alfred who died of croup at the age of three. Although there would be room for plenty more, the crypt has now been resealed. It will not be needed again because the family fell on hard times in the 20th century and moved away. Alderley New Hall, their sixty-bedroom house, burned down and the estate was sold to AstraZeneca.

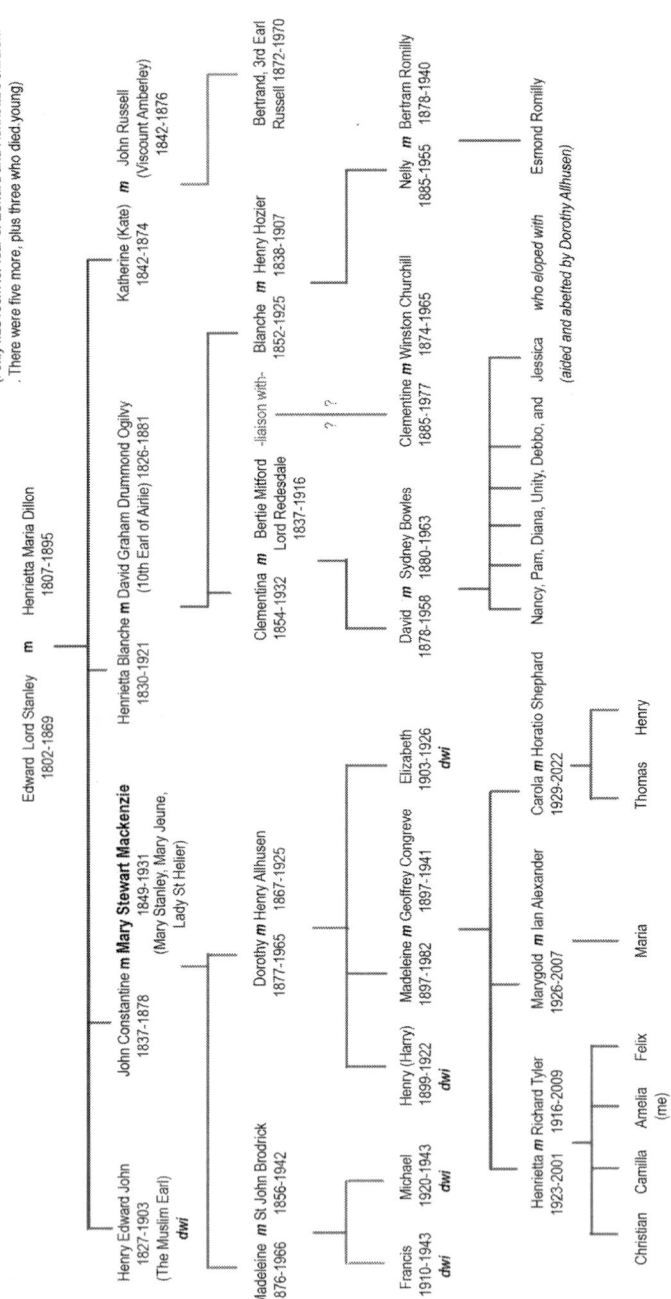

Not for the Faint-hearted

In which Mary's marriage to Johnny Stanley involves a Wild West adventure, and saddling her daughters with men's names

Life with Johnny was never going to be that smooth. In fact it's probably fair to say that the few years they spent together continued the process of 'hardening and bracing' that had begun with Mary's Highland upbringing. Although his soldiering days were over, when they married he had just returned from being in the thick of the Paris Commune, the world's first socialist revolution, and one of its shortest. Not that Johnny would ever have described himself as a socialist – he was there as an observer, not a fighter – but he had to admit to some support for the Communards' aims: 'I have got into a strong unreasonable sort of sympathy with the best of the Reds. They are fighting for municipal liberties – what all our towns have always enjoyed'. He also expressed unfettered admiration for the feisty female rebels he encountered during his stay. He wrote a full account, complete with grisly details, in letters to his mother which are quoted many times in Alastair Horne's book *The Fall of Paris, The Siege and the Commune 1870-71*.

The revolution ended abruptly with *la Semaine Sanglante*, when thousands of Communards were mercilessly gunned down in the streets of Paris, and Johnny returned to England. Three months later he and Mary were married, and moving into London's slightly unfashionable Wimpole Street. They had barely signed the lease and moved in the furniture when Mary found herself packing for a trip to America. Johnny was on the board of the Emma Silver Mine Company of Utah, and disturbing reports about it were reaching London. The shares had started to plummet, and someone was needed quickly to go and investigate. And so it was that Mary found

herself, with Johnny, aboard a steamship bound from Liverpool to New York.

An Atlantic crossing was still quite an undertaking in those days, and Mary had never been further west than Ireland. Technological improvements had reduced the journey time to just over a week – assuming favourable weather – but there were still more masts than funnels on the deck, in case the coal ran out. The object of the Stanleys' trip was supposed to be top secret, but somehow it leaked out, at which it became clear that a large number of their fellow passengers were bound on similar missions: 'mining experts, engineers, explorers, and an endless number of people interested in mining ventures seemed to spring from all parts of the ship', she records. It was the time of a great mining boom in the midwest of America, and the Emma mine was about to be exposed as one of the greatest swindles of the century. A certain Baron Albert Grant had managed to persuade British investors to part with some five million dollars which they would never see again. If they had only taken the trouble to check out the roguish 'Baron' they could have discovered that he had a ten-year history of setting up companies which collapsed, not to mention several allegations of fraud.

On arrival in New York, the urgent nature of their mission

meant that Mary and Johnny only had time for a quick drive around Central Park before continuing their journey west. They passed through Chicago just after the great fire which had killed 300 people, and left more than 100,000 residents homeless. She describes the grim sight in her memoir. 'There was nothing to be seen but a bare, black extent of land…broken here and there by the blackened skeletons of dwellings…the frames of which stood up gaunt and spectre-like against the skies.' Nothing was open, and Mary and Johnny grew more and more hungry as they searched among the ruins for somewhere to eat. Eventually they managed to find a little wooden shanty run by a pair of Chinese men, who miraculously produced a full English breakfast for them out of their last supplies.

They continued by train towards Salt Lake City, a journey of 12,000 miles. Utah had only recently been connected by rail with the East and a brand new Union Pacific bridge now spanned the Missouri. The Chief Engineer, who happened to be on board, invited the newly-weds to get down from the train and cross by foot, the better to admire it. What the train lacked in speed, 30 mph being the maximum, it made up for in style. The sleeping compartments were comfortable, the dining cars luxurious. Mark Twain describes them as being like hotels on wheels: 'tables covered with snowy linen, garnished with services of solid silver, and Ethiop waiters flitting about in spotless white.'

On arrival in Salt Lake City Mary was favourably impressed. Mormon pioneers had built it a mere 25 years earlier, but the mining boom had brought great prosperity. It was 'unlike any American town we had seen, with its well-paved streets, through which ran streams of water, flanked with trees on either side.'

The Emma Mine was in Little Cottonwood Canyon, high in the hills. Mary's worst fears were confirmed when they arrived to inspect the 'miserable, broken down deserted workings which were the only remains of this unlucky Eldorado.' The workforce of a hundred men had shrunk to only ten; it was, says Mary, a 'sucked orange'. A British miner who worked in the Emma later reported having seen silver ore 'plastered or engrafted onto the side of the limestone rock' to show to prospective investors – but there was no silver left to extract. There had been a landslide two days before and the mine had filled with water, so there was nothing to be done but return to Salt Lake City and await developments.

To kill time, Johnny and Mary called on The Prophet, Brigham Young, President of The Church of Jesus Christ of Latter-day Saints, or Mormons. Mary met some of his twenty wives, but the latest and most favourite wife refused to see her, evidently fearing (quite rightly) that in this British woman's eyes she would be seen as no better than a mistress. Mary also met Fanny Warn Stenhouse, soon to be famous for seceding from the Church and writing a bestseller that would invoke fury among the faithful: *Tell it All: the Story of a Life's Experience in Mormonism*. Fanny explained the system of polygamy to her, but Mary had a simpler theory. Getting domestic help in Utah was practically impossible: the Mormons had found a perfect solution to the Servant Problem.

It soon became clear that nothing could be done about the Emma mine. It remained flooded and today provides the water supply for the nearby town of Alta, a popular ski resort. Mary and Johnny decided to leave Salt Lake City and continue by stagecoach across the Sage Desert, Nevada. A long and gritty journey ended at a remote mining camp where, Mary claims, no white woman had hitherto been seen. There being no bath in the 'hotel', they went out in the early morning to a hot spring where you could bathe behind a piece of sheeting. Mary stood guard while Johnny bathed, then took her turn. But when she was ready to get out, naughty Johnny had wandered off – with her clothes. Meanwhile all around she could hear increasing signs of life as miners set off to work. If this was Johnny's idea of a joke, she took it in good part: 'after about five minutes of agony he returned... and I never felt happier than when I got into them again.'

They visited other mining camps where she found 'a wild,

picturesque, dare-devil lot of men – reckless, extravagant, and absolutely without any moral sense of right and wrong.' Clearly a far cry from Wimpole St. They arrived in Denver the night that a man had 'made a bet with some of his friends that he would ride down the street in his night-shirt, and let each of them have a shot at him, without being wounded... Every man at the windows and verandas of the hotel shot at him as he tore madly by, but he got to the winning post unhit and unharmed...' You couldn't get much more Wild West than that.

An eighteen-hour stagecoach ride took them through country where there was 'neither water, trees, nor vegetation of any kind – nothing but glaring sun; while the dust which our coach threw up was blown about by the wind in storms and clouds, filling our eyes and nostrils...' After this it was a relief to get back to the relative comfort of the train, visiting San Francisco, Yosemite, the East Coast, and finally spending a fortnight in Canada before sailing home aboard the White Star liner *Adriatic*. It was a stormy passage; two propellor blades broke and there was a head-wind all the way. With characteristic fortitude Mary remarks; 'Bad sailor as I was, the roughness and danger of that journey entirely cured me of my sea-sickness.'

The following year Johnny took Mary to Paris to see the devastation left in the aftermath of the Commune. They stayed at the hotel Mirabeau where Johnny had lodged, they visited the incinerated Jardin des Tuileries, and the Place Vendôme where Johnny had watched Napoleon's bronze column being hauled to the ground. He had come home with a piece of it in his pocket. In the Champs Elysées Mary saw houses still 'with broken windows, with no roofs, and an air of terrible desolation, and the *débris* of beautiful decorative furniture and hangings scattered everywhere.'

After that it was time to settle down in Wimpole Street, described by Thackeray as a 'dingy mausoleum of the genteel'. It formed part of the Portland Estate, whose owner was possibly

the most eccentric aristocrat of the century. William John Cavendish-Scott-Bentinck, 5th Duke of Portland, spent many years and most of his fortune constructing extensive chambers and tunnels under Welbeck Abbey, his country seat in Nottinghamshire. The Stanleys however would not have met him, as he was a pathological recluse, conducted all his business by post, and only went out under cover of darkness.

Before long a daughter came along. Johnny insisted that the baby be called after Thomas Carlyle, the 'sage of Chelsea'. Carlyle was something of a cult figure in his lifetime, recorded by posterity variously as a philosopher, a satirist, a fascist, and a sham. He was a friend of Johnny's family, 'though it can hardly be said that he sympathised with any of their opinions,' says Mary, 'except with those of Colonel Stanley [Johnny], who was a strong Conservative.' Carlyle had upset liberal sensibilities (but presumably not Johnny's) with his 1853 pamphlet *Occasional Discourse on the Nigger Question*, in which he lamented the abolition of slavery. He was a renowned misogynist, and his wife Jane had once warned Mary, 'My dear, whatever you do, never marry a philosopher'.

Johnny invited him to be Madeleine's godfather but his response was not over-enthusiastic: 'If you wish it, I am agreeable, only would you not like to wait for another time, when the boy you want may perchance make his tardy entry?' Johnny did not want to wait, instead christening the new baby Madeleine Cecilia Carlyle Stanley. Carlyle did not attend the christening, but he did like to come and spend the evening with the Stanleys in Wimpole Street where he would make Mary sing 'Scotch' songs to him. He would chuckle at *The Laird of Cockpen* and cry at *John Anderson, my Jo*.

Another person who enjoyed coming round to hear her 'Scotch songs and Irish melodies' was Alfred Lord Tennyson, who rented a house in Wimpole Street for a while. She and Johnny had first met him on a train journey to visit Johnny's sister Rosalind at Naworth Castle in Cumbria. In his rush to catch the train Tennyson had burnt his mouth on a breakfast of hot bread and milk, and spent the journey and the whole of the ensuing weekend complaining about it. 'Like many great men,' comments Mary, 'he bore small misfortunes with much less heroism than more serious ones.'

A year after Madeleine's birth another girl arrived, Osma Mary Dorothy, only ever known as Dorothy. This time it was a military hero of Johnny's who provided the peculiar name: Osman Pasha, field marshal of the Ottoman Empire. A month before Dorothy was born Pasha had boldly defended the Turkish city of Plevna against the Russians. Carlyle would not have approved of this choice of name. He was in the habit of venting tirades of abuse about the 'unspeakable Turk', not only to Mary and his other visitors, but also to the general public on the Chelsea omnibus, where the conductors had become quite used to it.

It is hard to know whether Mary was happy with Johnny. She is unfailingly loyal to him in her memoir, but Nancy Mitford says that he 'bullied her mercilessly'. Nancy also says that he became 'curmudgeonly' in his later years. This won't have been helped by the fact that Johnny was suffering from what was then called Bright's disease, a condition causing inflammation of the kidneys, apoplexy and convulsions. The medical treatments offered sound almost as unpleasant as the illness, as they included blood-letting and the administering of mercury and laxatives. None of these saved Johnny from a painful death at the age of 40, leaving Mary with two little daughters aged two and one. They had been married for seven years.

It may be remembered that Henry Stanley, the Muslim earl, had tried to stop Mary from installing a memorial to Johnny in the church at Alderley. However he reckoned without her determination. She took Henry to court, and won her case. Now the memorial, a bas-relief tablet, hangs in the chancel, boasting Johnny's deployment in Crimea in 1855. Mary was perhaps not aware that he was in Crimea for less than a month, most of which time was spent having dysentery. But her successful court case yielded more than a mere moral victory. Fighting Mary's corner was a barrister named Francis Jeune – over the course of the litigation they fell in love, and Mary married him.

Flirting with Socialism

In which Mary is admired for the 'width of her sympathies' as revolutionaries flock to her drawing room

A name that is conspicuously absent from Mary's memoir, and indeed largely unknown today, is that of Henry Mayers Hyndman. As the founder of Britain's first socialist party, you might expect him to at least have a niche on some iconostasis along with Marx and Lenin, but very few left-wingers today seem to be aware of his existence. His plunge into obscurity is probably due to the rapid disillusionment and defection of his followers, as Hyndman proved himself to be an imperious, and really rather absurd socialist leader.

Although he gets no mention in Mary's book, Hyndman's *Record of an Adventurous Life* devotes several pages to her. He thought she was wonderful. He lived in Devonshire Street, just round the corner from the Stanleys, and was a frequent visitor to their house in Wimpole Street. Expressing great admiration at 'the width of her sympathies', he records an evening that Mary spent with him before her second marriage.

> She sat up quite late one night at our house singing Jacobin songs of the old time, in alternation with revolutionary ditties from Prince Kropotkin, having quite possibly listened earlier in the day to the animated conversation of an ultra-Conservative like Lord Halsbury.

Hyndman himself was nothing if not a bundle of contradictions. His wardrobe made no concessions to his ideology, and he could regularly be seen on the Strand selling his magazine *Justice*, or haranguing a group of workers, dressed in a silk-faced tailcoat and top hat, every inch the caricature of a capitalist.

Hyndman was the son of a rich businessman, a graduate of Trinity College Cambridge and a cricket blue. He started out as a conservative and was a good friend of Johnny Stanley's – like him, he was on the board of directors of the dodgy Emma Silver Mine Company. The cataclysmic collapse of the Emma mine required him to travel to America more than once, and it was on one of these trips that he experienced his Damascene conversion. A friend had given him a French translation of *Das Kapital* just before he left England, and he spent much of his time in Salt Lake City reading it. At the same time he came across Henry George's best-seller *Progress and Poverty*, and these two books made such an impression on him that he vowed to set up a socialist party on his return to England.

In 1881 the Democratic Federation was born, attracting such early members as Eleanor Marx, George Bernard Shaw, and Frank Harris. Hyndman's private income from stocks and shares paid for the premises and a secretary. He was the first person to translate *Kapital* into English, though some curious timidity made him publish it under a pseudonym, John Broadhouse. It was received with derision by Engels, who reviewed it under the title 'How not to translate Marx'.

It was at one of Mary's parties that Hyndman first met Joseph Chamberlain, who at that time was regarded by many as a dangerous radical – he was known as 'the English Robespierre'. Lady Dorothy Nevill, who also met Chamberlain at Mary's, and immediately bonded with him over a shared obsession with orchids, recorded in her reminiscences that 'many of my old friends were quite alarmed lest I should become wildly revolutionary or something of that sort, for all sorts of absurd rumours used to be circulated as to the fierce communism of the rising politician…'.

Chamberlain had no public school or university education but had started out working in his uncle's screw factory when he was eighteen.

He turned it into a successful business before becoming Mayor of Birmingham, when he brought the town's services into public control, and in three years transformed it from a collection of filthy slums into a streamlined modern city. He was openly contemptuous of the aristocracy, once promising a crowd of demonstrators in Hyde Park that 'we will never, never, never be the only race in the civilised world subservient to the insolent pretensions of a hereditary caste'. Nevertheless he was happy enough to hang out with Mary's grand friends, Lady Dorothy being a case in point.

There is no doubt that Chamberlain was a charismatic man: handsome, arrogant, with a monocle on his face and an orchid in his buttonhole. Mary had got to know him shortly after Johnny's death, when her mother-in-law Henrietta Stanley had asked her who in the world she would most like to be introduced to. She had no hesitation in choosing Chamberlain, joyfully recalling the moment of their first meeting in her memoir: 'My wish was gratified and my pleasure was enhanced by the fact that he took me down to dinner.' Thirty years later she was still confessing to 'a deep feeling of affectionate personal friendship for him'.

When Hyndman met Chamberlain at Mary's, he expected to find plenty in common with the man who had so stirringly lamented the loss of public rights to land in his speech to the Birmingham Artisan's association:

> Some of them have been sold, some of them have been given away by people who had no right to dispose of them; some of them have been lost through apathy and ignorance; some have been stolen by fraud; and some have been acquired by violence... What ransom will property pay for the security it enjoys, what substitute will it find for the natural rights which have ceased to be recognised?

This speech was greeted with loud cheers, while the establishment interpreted his use of the word ransom as a seditious threat.

When Hyndman found himself sitting next to 'ransom' Chamberlain in Mary's drawing room, the hot topic was Irish land reform. Chamberlain was holding forth about fair rents, a subject he knew 'all there was to know about and a little more',  according to Hyndman. When challenged, Chamberlain started to get angry: 'his pistol having missed fire,' Hyndman says, he 'tried to knock me down with the butt-end.' As the argument grew more heated, polite conversation around them died away. Mary's other guests, who included some well-landed gentry, gaped at the sight of these two politicians, each as arrogant as the other, locking horns – 'so unusual in a fashionable drawing-room', said Hyndman.

It conjures up a dramatic picture: Chamberlain suave, smooth-shaven, with his signature monocle, and Hyndman sporting a patrician beard which reached down to his gold watch fob. For years to come, Hyndman said, he was reminded of that evening at Mary's whenever he bumped into people who had been there: 'Do you remember when Mr Chamberlain and you? etc etc'

An even longer-lasting spat kicked off some years later, when Henry George was invited by Mary to give a 'drawing-room talk' at her Harley Street home. George had recently become world-famous through his book *Progress and Poverty*, which in America was second in readership only to the Bible, and sold millions of copies worldwide. George advocated a tax on land to replace the tax on working men's wages, an idea that no-one ever seems to have found fault with apart from those who own large swathes of land.

Hyndman was bowled over by the book and invited George to stay, possibly unprepared for spending time with a man who had been destitute for the first forty years of his life, often reduced to begging on the street. He was mortified when George insisted on buying some whelks from a cockney costermonger's stall, and eating them then and there on the pavement, while Hyndman, who was a fine diner, looked on in embarrassment.

At Mary's gathering George was thrilled to see Alfred Lord Tennyson, looking 'tall and dreamy', and Robert Browning, looking more like 'a prosperous merchant draper.' But he was even more excited to have the opportunity to talk with Herbert Spencer, the famous evolutionary philosopher who George naturally assumed would share his beliefs. After all, was this not the man who had written 'Equity does not permit property in land'?

Spencer cut to the chase by asking George what he thought of the Irish Question, and George answered by roundly condemning the British Government and praising the Irish National Land League, many of whose supporters were currently in prison. To his astonishment, Spencer came back with: 'They have only got what they deserve. They are inciting people to refuse to pay to their landlords what is rightfully theirs – rent.' Henry George was deeply shocked by this reply. 'It is evident that we cannot agree on this matter,' he said stiffly, and turned away in disgust. After the encounter he wrote to a friend: 'Discount Herbert Spencer. He is most horribly conceited.' He followed this up with a whole book, *A Perplexed Philosopher*, which he devoted to denouncing Spencer. It was savage, attacking him as a traitor to the people and accusing him of 'intellectual prostitution.' If he wanted to upset the man, he certainly succeeded. Spencer invested considerable effort in defending himself in print, claiming that he had been misunderstood – but George now commanded an immense following, and Spencer continued to be misunderstood.

On a lighter note, one day Mary decided to prepare a socialist tea party specially to entertain Violet Paget, a gender-fluid friend of Oscar Wilde's. Violet was a multi-faceted intellectual, a lesbian and a pacifist, who wrote under the pen name Vernon Lee. Her subjects included aesthetics, the history of art and music, political philosophy, travel, and ghost stories. She dressed like a boy. Henry James said she was 'as dangerous and uncanny as she is intelligent, which is saying a great deal.'

At Mary's socialist party Violet was introduced to Henry Hyndman, of course, whom she described as a 'cock-a-whoop man', and, perhaps more surprisingly, Sergei Stepniak, an authentic Russian revolutionary. He was not only a revolutionary but an assassin, having killed the head of Russia's Secret Police with a dagger in the streets of St Petersburg not ten years earlier. He couldn't very well stay in Russia after that, and had escaped to Switzerland for a while before ending up in London. To be fair, he had given up violent struggle by the time he came to Mary's for tea, and was now contenting himself with writing and lecturing. He seems to have got away scot-free with his act of murder, but he did eventually come to a sticky if mundane end, getting run over by a train in Chiswick in 1895.

Mary never assumed that people with opposing political views could not get on with each other, however many times she was proved wrong. She was keen to introduce a 'Liberal agitator' friend of hers (unnamed) to Lord Edward Lytton, viceroy of India. Mary did not know Lytton that well, but believed that no-one 'could fail to succumb to his wonderful charm'. When Lytton rudely refused an introduction, in the presence of her 'socialist friend', the scales fell from her eyes. Lytton was not popular in India. During the great famine of 1876, when somewhere between 6 and 9 million people died, he oversaw the export of a record 320,000 tons of Indian wheat to England. He referred to the natives as 'Bengalee Baboos' and only narrowly escaped assassination.

Hyndman's friendship with Mary continued into her second marriage. In 1886 he was charged with inciting the Black Monday riots in London's West End. Still in his top hat and tails, he had roused the crowd in Trafalgar Square with an inflammatory speech, winding up with: 'Follow me to the West End to demand work, bread or blood!' A mob of some ten thousand unemployed workers made their way towards Hyde Park via Pall Mall and St James, smashing the windows of gentlemen's clubs as they went, while well-heeled Tories rained insults on them from the upper floors. Hyndman was arrested but released on bail, and he came to Francis Jeune to get some legal advice. 'Whatever you do, Hyndman,' said Francis, 'defend yourself and speak last. Don't be brilliant. On the contrary be a trifle dull. Interest them in your career.' Hyndman ignored this advice, instead using the courtroom as a platform to hold forth on the condition of London's poor, and to deliver his socialist views. He was acquitted!

Many of these people have sunk into obscurity. Spencer took up an anti-socialist stance and became increasingly isolated and hypochondriac in old age. Vernon Lee's brilliance was too varied to nail a specific audience, although some attempt has recently been made to revive interest in her work. Henry George was way ahead of his time, suggesting that one of the houses of Congress should be filled with women. When he died, just shy of 60 years old, his funeral attracted 200,000 mourners. After which his name gradually faded from view, although his system of land tax has been partially adopted in Australia, Taiwan, and Singapore, and in some American states.

As for Hyndman, he, like Chamberlain, became increasingly jingoistic as he got older, and the Social Democratic Federation lost many followers who objected to his autocratic style of leadership. Perhaps it was Mary's publishers who did not want the frock-coated leftie included in her memoir, for she remained a loyal friend. When he died, in 1922, she set up a Hyndman Memorial Committee which included George Bernard Shaw (who had long since defected from the Democratic Federation), Thomas Hardy, and 'many prominent Social Democrats, Socialists, and Labour men', according to the Portsmouth Evening News. Together they commissioned a bronze bust of Hyndman which was donated to the National Portrait Gallery.

Francis Jeune

In which Mary finds happiness in her second marriage

Francis was a nice man. My aunt told me that his stepdaughters, Madeleine and Dorothy, were very fond of him. He eventually became the chief divorce lawyer of Great Britain, which may seem ironic given Mary's stout support of the institution of marriage. But then that was no doubt due to the happiness she found with him. Francis was kind, clever, and hardworking. His character is perhaps best described in this passage from the oddly eponymous book *Sir Arthur Conan Doyle*, by Sir Arthur Conan Doyle:

> Another distinguished man of the law who left a very clear impression upon my mind was Sir Francis Jeune, afterwards Lord St Helier. I attended several of Lady Jeune's famous luncheon parties, which are quite one of the outstanding institutions of London, like Gladstone's breakfasts, in the last quarter of the nineteenth century. I am indebted to this lady for very many kind actions. Her husband always impressed me with his gentle wisdom and with his cultivated taste. He told me that if every copy of Horace were destroyed he thought that he could reconstruct most of it from memory. He presided over the Divorce Courts, and I remember upon one occasion I said to him: "You must have a very low opinion of human nature, Sir Francis, since the worst side of it is forever presented towards you." "On the contrary," said he very earnestly, "my experience in the Divorce Courts has greatly raised my opinion of humanity. There is so much chivalrous self-sacrifice and so much disposition upon the part of everyone to make the best of a bad business that it is extremely edifying".

Francis' approach to divorce was enlightened. He liked to advise temporary separation as a cure for marital problems, and he was the first person to propose mediation in the form of conciliation courts. He had earned scholarships to Harrow and Balliol, and then worked for the law firm of Baxter, Rose, and Norton, solicitors to Disraeli. The most exciting thing that he had done before he met Mary was getting involved in the Tichborne Claimant affair, which culminated in one of the longest cases ever to be heard in a British court, and divided public opinion to an almost violent degree.

A short time after Mary and Francis wed they found themselves at a dinner party where some young man was boasting that he was sure he'd been to a more remote outpost than anyone else round the table. When he mentioned the name of the place – Wagga Wagga – he was astonished to be told that Francis had also been there, at more or less the same time as himself. Wagga Wagga in New South Wales is today a city of about 60,000 people, but at that time, before the arrival of the railway, it was little more than a village. To reach it required a journey of 'many long, weary days.' Francis had been dispatched there by his firm to check out the claim of a corpulent butcher, one Thomas Castro, that he was the heir to the Tichborne title and estate.

How this came about is as follows: Roger Tichborne, the rightful heir, was lost in a shipwreck in 1854. His mother refused to accept that he was dead, and convinced herself that he had survived and made his way to Australia. She advertised extensively in the Australian press, and eventually, in 1866, this Thomas Castro stepped forward claiming to be her lost son. She accepted him immediately, but the rest of the family had their doubts. Roger had spent his childhood in France and spoke French as a first language. Castro had a cockney accent and couldn't understand a word of French, nor could he tell Latin from Greek, both of which Roger had studied at school. Francis was satisfied that he was an imposter.

With the help of financial support from his 'mother', Castro returned to England and tried to evict the man who was renting Tichborne Park in Hampshire, one Colonel Lushington. In the civil case of 1871 Francis acted as counsel for the tenant (who, strangely, nevertheless believed that Castro was Roger). Much of the evidence Francis produced was aimed at proving that Castro was an imposter, and that he was really Arthur Orton, a butcher's son from Wapping. The jury confidently rejected Castro/Orton's suit, whereupon he was charged with perjury and bundled into Newgate Prison to await a criminal case. This was to last for nearly a year and fill a whole page of the Times every day in the summer of 1873.

But there was a lot of public support for Castro. As George Bernard Shaw wrily remarked, it was an absurd paradox, 'whereby the Claimant was perceived simultaneously as a legitimate baronet and as a working-class man denied his legal rights by a ruling elite'. Ordinary people took against the heavy-handed way in which the judge instructed the jury. Besides, there was Andrew Bogle, a trusted family servant of the Tichbornes who had been rescued by Roger's father from a slave plantation in Jamaica and had spent a lot of time with the boy as he was growing up. He swore to his dying day that Castro was the real deal. Whether Bogle was duped by the Claimant or collaborating with him depends on which side you want to take. Bogle's son Henry sat next to Castro throughout the trial, as can be seen in the beautifully detailed painting by Frederick Sargent (see page 58). Castro's generously-proportioned face occupies the focal centre of the picture, young Bogle at his side, while Francis Jeune, with his long straight nose and matching beard, can be seen on the far left.

Marriage to Francis brought many benefits to Mary. For a start, she now had a husband who earned a wage, which gave her freedom to pursue her social studies of East End life and to record them for the periodical press. It also provided a large and comfortable country house in Berkshire which had been bought some years earlier by Francis' mother. Now Mary had the use of Arlington

Manor, and could take the family and as many guests as she wanted at the weekends.

After the Tichborne case Francis' workload was relatively humdrum. Thanks to the Matrimonial Causes Act of 1857, and its sequel the Married Women's Property Act of 1882, divorce rates were gradually rising. In 1880 there were about three hundred cases; by the end of the century the annual number had doubled and these, along with his probate work, kept Francis busy. But he did preside over another *cause celèbre* in 1892, when the scandalous 'Duchess Blair' stood in the dock.

Described by the press as 'six feet tall, raw-boned, and grim-featured', Mary Caroline Blair was the epitome of a Victorian anti-heroine. Her scandalous activities were fourfold (or possibly five). She started out by conducting a lengthy affair with her husband's employer, the Duke of Sutherland. When Mr Blair died in a shooting 'accident', it provoked much speculation as to whether it was indeed an accident. The affair continued until the Duke's wife died, whereupon Caroline married him – after a shocking four months, instead of the conventional year of mourning. When the Duke died, leaving her most of his property, his children from the first marriage contested the will. It was at this point that Caroline made a signal error – in the presence of solicitors who were examining the case, she threw some papers into the fire and burned them.

This gave Francis enough grounds to convict her of contempt of court and send her to Holloway prison – a singular experience for any duchess. However she did get a luxury cell, and on her release did a deal with the family whereby she relinquished her claim in return for enough money – in cash – to build Carbisdale Castle (now a luxury hotel) adjacent to the Sutherland estate.

It can't be said that Mary was in any way dependent on her husband's contacts for her social success, which was already established. Letters of introduction were keenly sought by those who were not yet on her guest list. Theodore Roosevelt (largely responsible for Britain's 'special relationship' with America) turned up clutching one such letter. Mary took to him at once, noting: 'rather short-sighted, with keen blue eyes, fine strong head, and the most wonderful teeth I have ever seen in my life'. They kept in touch for many years, later exchanging condolences on the losses of their sons. Another time he wrote: 'I shall always remember the pleasure you gave me' – but on reading it through hastily amended it to 'the pleasure your kindness gave me' in case anyone should get the wrong impression.

Francis' profession did provide Mary with some unusual opportunities, one of which was visiting the workings of the first Channel Tunnel. Francis had as a client the railway entrepreneur Edward Watkin, whose long-term vision was to join Manchester to Paris by rail. He had already started boring the tunnel, which so far was about a mile long. His method of gaining support for the project was to invite people like William Gladstone and the Archbishop of Canterbury to champagne receptions in the tunnel, and so it was that one day in 1881 Mary and Francis travelled down to Dover with various bankers, lawyers, and MPs on a special train from Charing Cross. The entire party was taken down into the tunnel 'to watch the great revolving drill piercing through the chalk, which was carried away in small trucks.' After that they were drawn up again and treated to a slap-up lunch.

But the good people of England were very averse to the idea of connecting their country to the Continent. It was obvious to them that it would only encourage invasion by foreigners, and so despite the high-profile guests the project was quashed. The original entrance to Watkin's tunnel works can still be seen in the face of Shakespeare Cliff near Dover.

In 1891 Francis was made President of the Probate, Divorce and Admiralty division, and knighted. Mary now became Lady Jeune. The following year Gladstone appointed him Judge Advocate General, giving him jurisdiction over court-martials. That same year Mary attended what was possibly the most bizarre event of her life: the unique broadcast of Cardinal Manning's voice from 'beyond the grave'.

Mary had had various dealings with the cadaverous prelate, finding herself fascinated but somewhat repelled by Manning's 'ascetic, bloodless face, with the keen, watchful eyes, which hid every emotion or feeling'. She had met him a few times in connection with rescue work, but also 'for personal reasons' – probably to do with him receiving her brother-in-law Algernon Stanley into the Catholic church back in 1879. Manning had outraged the Church of England by his own conversion many years earlier. It was an action which in those days was viewed as deeply unpatriotic.

Manning had a strong rival in the form of Cardinal Newman, another controversial convert to Catholicism. In the long term Newman won the holy struggle for power, by getting canonised in 2019, but back then it was Manning who had clawed his way to the superior position, his mind closed, the *Catholic Herald* said, 'like a steel trap on faith.' When Manning was asked to give his opinion on Newman's *Apologia* (regarded by the faithful as a work equal in stature to the *Confessions of St Augustine*) he said coldly, 'It is like listening to the voice of one from the dead.' So it is curious that when Manning lay dying he was offered the chance to compete with Newman quite literally, by using the latest technology – Edison's phonograph – to record some spoken words.

After his death an odd collection of thirty or so people who had known Manning was summoned to Whitehall Court, a block of luxury flats on the Embankment, to hear the recording. The gathered group listened with bated breath to the faint scratching of the phonograph, but the message when it came, accompanied by a slight buzzing noise, was an anti-climax: 'To all who come after me; I hope that no words of mine, written or spoken in my life, will be found to have done harm to anyone after I am dead – Henry Edward Manning, Cardinal Archbishop.' Mary simply found it 'weird and uncanny,' and not at all the solemn occasion she had been expecting. Nevertheless someone thought it worth photographing for posterity.

A somewhat fuzzy photo from Mary's memoir – still you can see that she is, unsurprisingly, centre stage

But back to the Jeune home: a happy event was the birth of Francis junior, a brother for Madeleine and Dorothy. Less happy was the fact that he barely survived to manhood. In August 1904, aged 22 and serving as ADC to Lord Lamington in India, he contracted typhoid fever. Within three weeks he was dead. Many Europeans suffered the same fate in Poona (now Pune), which is set in a cup-like hollow that allows foul air to stagnate. A contemporary report says: 'The pit and trench systems of sewerage are open [sic!] to many objections, having had the most disastrous effects upon the health of British troops and civil residents quartered in the cantonments.' Although a vaccine for typhoid had been developed in 1896, until WW1 it was only administered to soldiers who volunteered themselves, and presumably young Francis had not.

Francis Jeune senior, never a strong man himself, was overcome with grief at their loss. His health deteriorated rapidly, forcing his resignation from the Probate, Divorce and Admiralty Division in January 1905. The following month he was raised to the peerage, with the title Baron St Helier. Born a Jerseyman, Francis was anxious that Hélier should be spelt correctly, with an accent on the first e. George Morrison, *Times* correspondent, recounts the response of the Garter King at Arms to this demand:

> He said that there was no accent in the British Peerage. 'But St Hélier is a town in the British Empire', said Jeune. 'I have nothing to do with the British Empire – there is and there shall be no accent in the British Peerage.' So after all he had to forgo the accent. Shortly afterwards he died, going let us hope to a place where his accent may be allowed him.

Francis Senior followed his son to the grave after only 10 months, in April of 1905. In response to a letter of condolence Mary Jeune, now Lady St Helier, wrote:

> We have had twenty-three years of perfect happiness, and until our boy died last year, we never had a cloud on our sky... I dare not dwell on what his loss is to me, for that would be impossible, and as we have been the most constant and inseparable companions all these long years, my desolation is very great.

Slumming

In which Mary teams up with an ex-pirate, hunts down slum landlords and mounts a landmark prosecution

It may come as a surprise to some to learn that in Victorian times rents per square foot in London's East End were no cheaper than they were in Belgravia. This was made possible by the simple strategy of cramming as many people into each square foot as was physically possible, and there was always a ready supply of ex-agricultural workers and Jewish refugees to keep East End houses bulging at the seams. Slumlords, also known as rent farmers, or 'vampyres of the poor' could make a tidy profit out of dwellings that weren't fit to house a pig – though they sometimes did that as well. Demolitions were ordered, but not carried out. Until, that is, Mary got involved with Mr Bennett Burleigh.

There were slums all over London, but the East End was home to the most notorious of the lot, the Old Nichol. And this was where Mary spent much of her time. In between organising parties and writing for the periodical press, she would be taking the penny omnibus from her comfortable home in Marylebone to the meanest streets of the capital. She went from house to house, taking notes and compiling statistics for her articles. Wherever she found a problem she tried to address it, spawning an impressive number of philanthropic projects, mostly designed to improve the quality of life for children.

Philanthropy at the time was a fashionable occupation for women of a certain class. In 1885 the *Times* reported that the revenue of London charities exceeded the GNP of Sweden, Denmark, or Portugal. This was followed by an article in the *Scottish Review* complaining that 'results are not what they should be, considering the enormous amount of both money and personal exertion expended.' Mary's Aunt Louisa was busy building seamen's missions in Canning Town, while her sister-in-law Maude Stanley pioneered youth work around Soho and founded a network of girls' clubs. But like many do-gooders of the time their aid came with strings attached. Both Louisa and Maude were temperance proselytisers, convinced that all the troubles of the poor could be blamed on alcohol.

Mary had a far more pragmatic approach, and was positively dismissive of 'the philanthropic gush of excellent people who have no practical knowledge of their subject.' She had started out working with the rehabilitation of 'fallen' women, inspired by Angela Burdett-Coutts, the 'Queen of the Poor', whom she had got to know in the 'sixties. The list of charities started by Angela would fill a page of this book, but she is perhaps best known for financing Dickens' Urania Cottage, the first rescue home where fallen women were treated with compassion rather than reproof. At the age of 23 Angela had inherited half the Coutts Bank fortune and become the richest woman in London after the Queen. By resisting all offers of marriage (and there were many) she retained power over her finances, and was thus able to give away more than £3 million in her lifetime.

Mary had no such resources to draw on but raised funds for her various projects herself, by repeated appeals in the press. This is an extract from a fairly typical letter she wrote to the *St James' Gazette* in 1886:

> The past winter and spring have been unusually severe, taxing to the utmost the resources of the poor in London and those who work among them; and none of the community have suffered more sorely than the children, to whom parents out of work and slackness of trade mean indescribable privations. The children are more poorly clad and worse shod this year than I ever remember them...

And every one who sends me money may like to know that it all goes to help the children, as I have no committee and no office, and all the work is done by myself.'

Her projects provided Christmas stockings, country holidays and boots for impoverished East End children. She was the manager of more than one school in the area, and a member of the General Purposes Committee of the People's Palace in Mile End Road. This huge building – now part of Queen Mary University – rivalled Alexandra Palace in North London and the Crystal Palace in the South, boasting a swimming pool, winter gardens, and lecture rooms which offered technical education for citizens of the East End. She started the Children's Holiday Fund with a sum of £500 which she winkled out of Henry Labouchère, one of the more contradictory characters of the era.

He came from a family wealthy enough that he could get away with all kinds of bad behaviour. While at Cambridge University he lost £6,000 gambling on horses, though this unsuccessful debut didn't deter him from devising a system for 'winning' at roulette which is still in use today. His anxious parents found him a job as a diplomat, which he managed to hold down for ten years in spite of being a total stranger to diplomacy. He started a magazine called *Truth*, devoted to exposing scandals and corruption, and to lambasting feminists, homosexuals, and Jews. His wealth allowed him to shrug off frequent libel cases. At the same time he had a kind of socialist, anti-imperialist agenda, and always published Mary's appeals for donations to the Holiday Fund in his magazine.

But Labouchère inspired animosity in many quarters. For twenty years he lived with an actress called Henrietta Hodson, thus scandalising society. Eventually he married her, and they were able to appear as a couple at one of Mary's dinner parties. However, the minute the newly-weds arrived another guest, the Lord High Chancellor of Great Britain, 'after a pained but not prolonged pause' got up and left, taking his wife with him and 'going home dinnerless'. Labouchère does NOT merit a mention in Mary's memoir.

He is best remembered today for his amendment to the 1885 Criminal Law Act which made 'gross indecency' a crime, and was responsible for seeing Oscar Wilde imprisoned for two years (Labouchère would have preferred it to be seven), and for ruining the lives of countless gay men thereafter. Still, by the time Oscar met his downfall Mary's Holiday Fund was sending over a thousand children to the country each year, and according to *Punch* magazine 'imparting incalculable happiness'.

Mary was a keen proponent of free school meals, or indeed, any school meals at all. Primary education had become universal in 1870 but, bizarrely, schools were not *allowed* to feed their pupils, and poor children were often too hungry to learn. Mary helped to set up the London School Dinners Association, for as she argued in an essay,

> If we insist on educating our children, and make their attendance at school compulsory, ought we not logically to go a step further, and insist on their being fed…? At a very small cost, children can be provided with a dinner of good soup and a large piece of bread…

Nothing much changed until the Provision of Meals Act of 1906 – and even then it wasn't mandatory. Meanwhile Mary's solution was to turn up in person three or four times a week during the winter months to administer hot meals to 700 odd children, with Madeleine and Dorothy helping as soon as they were old enough. She wasn't afraid of mucking in. A teacher at the Nichol Board School recalls her

> inspecting the meat and vegetables used, giving with her own hands the bread and soup to each child, not merely superintending but taking a most active part in the distribution.

Thomas Hardy also records her willingness to get hands on with catering, on a weekend jaunt from her country house:

We had a delightful picnic to Savernake Forest from Arlington – a party of about 10 – Lady J. cooked the luncheon at the picnic-house with the dexterity of a *chef*. [She] cooked luncheon in a great saucepan, with her sleeves rolled up and an apron on.'

The Nichol Board School was in the heart of the infamous Old Nichol, which lay between Bethnal Green Road and Columbia Road. The death rate here was nearly twice that of Bethnal Green as a whole. What had once been back gardens were now filled with tenements and workshops until they met the buildings in the next street. Some houses were only eight feet wide and many had no foundations, the floorboards being placed directly onto the earth, while leaky walls and roofs resulted in a sort of permanent indoor mist that was characteristic of Old Nichol dwellings.

As many as ninety people might be crammed into a ten-roomed house, not to mention various livestock: ducks, geese, even donkeys. Some of the houses had cellar passages underneath them, described by a contemporary medical officer as 'one of the most alarming architectural phenomena' of the district. These passages were about 5 feet high, dark and airless, and the only route to the back yard and lavatories – nevertheless they were sometimes illegally rented out as 'accommodation'. Many inhabitants of East End houses worked at home, French polishing, making boots or matchboxes, or breeding dogs and birds. Some took in washing, further adding to the dampness.

Mary visited many houses like these, and described them in great detail in her essay 'The Homes of the Poor' in *Fortnightly Review*. She condemned them as 'a disgrace to civilisation' – she recorded how much people earned and how much they paid in rent, and how they pawned their clothes and went without food rather than lose a roof, however porous, over their heads.

The neat fronts of the terraced houses gave no clue as to what lay behind. A house off Leather Lane in Clerkenwell had twelve rooms and contained twelve families. 'The moment the door was opened the effluvia from the bad drainage was sickening,' she wrote. In Newling Street Mary reported that 'the state of the dwellings was disgraceful beyond words... The spectacle of that back yard was one never to be forgotten. The dirt and dilapidation, the smell and the squalor, were indescribable; and the ruined closets without doors, many without walls, proclaimed the utter absence of any sense of decency or of cleanliness.'

The squalor had not gone unnoticed. Sensational press reports and even more sensational novels about life in 'the rookeries' attracted religious philanthropists, temperance campaigners, and political agitators. They also attracted tourists from the more prosperous parts of London who went 'slumming' as a leisure activity, peering with fascination, as though they were at the zoo, into the lives of fellow humans who somehow managed to live without any bed to sleep in nor any means of cooking a meal. No wonder the residents were suspicious of intruders, however well-meaning.

Many do-gooders entered homes with a temperance pledge book in their hands, though as Mary said: 'If a man and his family live in a room in which we would not kennel our dogs, need we wonder that the man seeks warmth and light at the public house?' Other visitors came armed with bibles, offering salvation from hell. 'There can be no hell hereafter', said one denizen of the Nichol, 'we live in it already.' Anti-landlord meetings in Victoria Park attracted thousands of listeners, but the rent strikes that were advocated did not catch on. Non-payment of rent led to eviction, the only place to go from there being 'up the road' – the Kingsland Road workhouse.

So what was to be done? A whole series of 'Nuisance Removal' acts had made inspection and demolition possible, but for nearly thirty years no successful actions had been taken against landlords. For one thing the acts were permissive – i.e. they were suggestions rather than laws. For another, as Mary pointed out, residents were 'too busy, too down-trodden, to resist, and even ignorant of the laws designed for their protection.' Thirdly, the parish vestries which preceded the establishment of a London County Council were riddled with corruption, the vestrymen often having an interest in the very properties they were responsible for inspecting.

Mary shared the beleaguered tenants' distrust of bureaucracy, and was not afraid to go on the attack. 'There can be no guarantee,' she wrote, 'with… the inherent love of jobbery that characterises the traditions of Bumbledom, that the men appointed to fill these posts are capable and honest.' (Jobbery is defined as 'the improper use of public office or conduct of public business for private gain'. The word seems to have faded from use, I can't think why.) And crowning all this was the widely-held view that a landlord's right to his property was sacrosanct, because an Englishman's home was his castle, even if he did not live in it himself but rented it out to as many people as he (or she) could cram into it.

It was not uncommon to find the poor blamed for their 'weaknesses and improvidence'. Mary fumed at this: 'Such criticisms make one burn with indignation,' she wrote. 'Nowhere do we come across such deeds of devotion, self-sacrifice, and heroism, as are witnessed among the humblest inhabitants of some of the most miserable alleys in London.'

But attitudes were changing, thanks partly to the brutal murders of several women in the Whitechapel area in the latter part of 1888. The Ripper's victims were women who had found themselves homeless for one reason or another, and had taken the risk of sleeping in the doorways or staircases of shared houses. George Bernard Shaw, then still relatively unknown, wrote a sarcastic letter to the *Star* newspaper:

> Whilst we conventional Social Democrats were wasting our time on education, agitation and organisation, some independent genius has taken the matter in hand, and by simply murdering

and disembowelling four women, converted the proprietary press to an inept sort of communism.

For years the establishment press had paid no attention to the causes of overcrowding and homelessness in slumland. Mary's findings from her own house-to-house investigations had been similarly passed over. 'There has been no class so much neglected,' she said, 'as that of the women who have to pick up a living in the daytime and have no recognised home at night.' Now however it was no longer possible to ignore the vulnerability of women who had no safe place to shelter.

In the autumn of 1889 a column appeared in the *Daily Telegraph* which echoed many of Mary's own findings. It was headed 'Justice for Workwomen', with the anonymous byline 'A Friend of the Poor', and it described in great detail the squalid conditions in which many East End women worked – i.e. in their own homes. Mary soon found out that the journalist behind this investigation was none other than Bennett Burleigh, acclaimed war correspondent of the *Telegraph*. He had famously made the scoop of the decade by using a sneaky trick: when General Gordon was assassinated at Khartoum, he got the telegraph operator to transmit the entire Book of Genesis, effectively keeping all the lines busy while he prepared his copy, and preventing other journalists from submitting theirs. On another occasion he threw a rival reporter's bags out of a train, forcing the man to leap out after them and allowing Burleigh to nab a prize interview before him.

His obituary when he died was twice as long as that of Alfred Lord Tennyson. 'He embraced his career', said the *Telegraph*, 'with the ardour of a lover'. Sadly, he didn't embrace his lovers with the same ardour – at least not for any length of time.

On the face of it Burleigh was a surprising companion for respectable Mary – to say that his past was colourful is something of an understatement. One can only assume that she was not aware that his behaviour had at times amounted to foul play, because I don't think she would have approved. He was born in Glasgow in 1840. At the age of twenty he got one of the family servants pregnant and was hauled up the aisle by his father, but it wasn't long before he abandoned his wife and took himself off to America, where the civil war was raging. His intention was to make money by selling a torpedo that his father had designed. He failed to interest the Union side, so then he offered it to the Confederates. They were suspicious, thinking that he might be a Union spy, and the only way he could convince them that he wasn't was by volunteering for them.

And so he became a pirate in the Chesapeake, disrupting Union shipping. He was quite successful at this until in 1864 he was captured by Union forces, sentenced to death and imprisoned on an island. He managed to escape by prising up the floorboards of his cell and swimming out through the sewage system and across the sea till he got to shore – a five-hour odyssey. Not long after that he was again caught hijacking a Union warship, but again he got away, escaping death for a second time.

He returned to Britain and took up work as a journalist, reporting from front lines in Egypt, Libya, South Africa and the Balkans (to name but a few), He married two more times, producing ten children over a period of four decades, and deserting their mothers. Where the sudden interest in poor women came from is hard to know. By the time he met Mary his own poor first wife had died in a workhouse in Glasgow.

Mary joined forces with Burleigh to instigate a case under the Nuisances Removal Act. The action they chose to finance and pursue was on behalf of three tenants of the so-called 'model tenements' of Ann's Place, Boundary Street. It must be said that 'Nuisances Removal' is a curiously mild term for what they had to deal with. The Ann's Place dwellings, just off Shoreditch High Street, housed 108 people in 33 rooms. They had been built over what had once been a garden, overshadowed by the surrounding high walls of houses and workshops, but nonetheless providing a little ventilation. Now, Mary writes, 'there was no air; the floors were full of rat holes; the walls were running down with damp; the sanitary arrangements were out of order; there was no regular supply of water...' and so on. Previous attempts had been made to close the tenements as unfit, but the landlord had successfully appealed the decision by promising to repair them, even though the Shoreditch medical officer stated in court that no amount of money would make the dwellings fit for human habitation. A flurry of papering and whitewashing had ensued, enough to satisfy the inspectors before the wetness soaked back through.

The difficulty of finding out who the landlord was posed another obstacle. Rent books did not have to reveal the identity of property owners, and in any case many of them were not even alive, the money being paid into the estates of the deceased, or getting leached into long drawn-out court cases, like Dickens' Jarndyce v. Jarndyce. Many landlords were aristocrats. Thirty-eight Nichol houses belonged to a Duke who also owned more than 10,000 acres of land in Britain. He had nearly as many names as he had properties: Richard Plantagenet Campbell Temple Nugent Brydges Chandos Grenville, Earl Temple of Stowe, Viscount and Baron Cobham, Lord Kinloss, Earl Nugent, third Marquis and Duke of Buckingham and Chandos.

Landlords like this often remained hidden behind their solicitor or leaseholder, whose agents would collect the rents. Meanwhile the agents, Mary writes, 'not only bully the tenants, but often take the law into their own hands, and turn the people into the streets without legal warrant of any kind.' Mary suggested that withholding rent might flush out the landlords, but Burleigh had to remind her that this was the last thing that tenants would agree to. Instead, he said, he would track them down via official correspondence. He was as good as his word – in less than 24 hours he succeeded in unearthing the landlords of Ann's Place who were, somewhat ironically, the National Temperance Land and Building Company.

The case took place at Worship Street magistrates court. The

Magistrate sitting in judgement was one Montagu Williams QC, luckily a man who was unusually sympathetic to the suffering of the poor. He records in his memoir how he went to inspect the dwellings himself, breaking quite uncharacteristically into several exclamation marks: 'Good Heavens! What a place it was! To think that one's fellow creatures were doomed to live in such filthy holes!' He had no hesitation in ordering the closure of the dwellings in Ann's Place, to be followed by their demolition.

The *Brewers Guardian* had a field day with the story. 'We do not think the 'temperance' gentry have much reason for self-gratulation,' they crowed. 'How much blood money in the form of rent has this Company been wringing out of the poor starved creatures who have lived – we mean existed – in such a fearful place?'

This first successful case created an important precedent, recorded with characteristic modesty by Mary in her essay 'The Homes of the Poor':

> Until recently it was always understood that only the tenants themselves could put the law in action. As a matter of fact it is open to anyone to move... The buildings closed by a magistrate's order in Ann's Court and Newling Street, Bethnal Green, were condemned on the application of an outsider.

She doesn't mention that the outsider was in fact herself, and indeed I would never have known this if it were not for Sarah Wise's delightfully readable book *The Blackest Streets*, subtitled *The Life and Death of a Victorian Slum*. When I asked for permission to use some of her material the author was kind enough to tell me that when she came across Mary Jeune she adored her, and that I had a 'fantastic relative'.

Mary Jeune and Bennett Burleigh now got together with the Bishop of Bedford and the Women's Trades Union and Provident League, and set up the Fair Rents for Healthy Homes League, with meetings in the Monarch coffee house in Bethnal Green Road. Tenants could bring their grievances which would then be reported in the *Telegraph*, thus outing and shaming landlords. This, and the success of the Ann's Place judgement, led to many more summonses being issued. East End neighbourhoods exploded with a ferment of whitewashing and wallpapering, but of course these superficial improvements were useless.

In 1888 the London County Council was established, and a couple of years later the Housing for the Working Classes Act was passed, giving the local authority powers of compulsory purchase. Slum clearance started in earnest. The Old Nichol was razed to the ground, and replaced by the world's first council estate, showcasing the red-brick Arts and Crafts tenements of Arnold Circus. They surround a central raised garden under which much of the rubble of the old Nichol remains buried.

Mary had her own firm ideas about the design of buildings that should replace the slums, and she sets them out in 'The Homes of the Poor'. They include 'soil pipes venting above the house' (essential) and 'glazed tiles as dados for stairs and rooms' (optional). But it would be another twenty years before she could add legislative clout to housing reform, when she became one of London County Council's first female aldermen.

The Theatre and Millicent Fawcett

In which Mary enjoys a very public disagreement with Millicent and her Social Purity vigilantes – but makes it up over Suffrage

Mary adored the theatre in all its forms, from Shakespeare to domestic farce. She never forgot her first experience of drama in Edinburgh, when she and her sister had shed buckets of tears over Dumas' *Catherine Howard: the Throne, the Scaffold and the Tomb*. She was partial to a bit of acting herself, and guests at her Arlington Manor weekends would often be entertained by the entire Jeune family putting on 'cup-and-saucer' dramas, complete with costume, music, and printed programmes. This love of theatre, combined with her preoccupation with child poverty, was to bring her into conflict with Millicent Fawcett and her army of feminist vigilantes.

When Mary first moved to London in the sixties, the theatre provided popular entertainment for the masses but was regarded as disreputable by the upper classes, and you would never meet an actor in Society. It wasn't until Henry Irving took over management of the Lyceum Theatre in 1878, in partnership with Ellen Terry, that it began to acquire some respectability. Irving was committed to elevating drama to high art, much aided by Terry who brought star quality to all the leading lady rôles. Needless to say, Irving and Terry soon became frequent visitors to Mary's house, and Terry encouraged the two girls to come down and visit the theatre.

Madeleine and Dorothy became regular attendants at the Lyceum, so much so that Irving and Terry provided them with special chairs in the wings so that they could get a really good view of proceedings. One night there was an important debate in the House of Commons from which Gladstone was conspicuous by his absence. This was commented on in the morning papers, and again at a luncheon party at Mary's, everyone speculating as to where he could have been. 'Oh,' piped up the girls, 'Mr Gladstone was with us at the Lyceum, behind the scenes; he was sitting in the big chair, and each of us had a little chair at his side.'

They loved Ellen Terry and called her Aunt Nellie. She had 'an extraordinarily bright, joyous nature', says Mary. 'Everyone, in fact, came under her charms', including Mary's Persian cats, who would 'wind themselves round her neck, and lie there purring the whole evening.' No doubt it was this charm that enabled Terry to get away with a rather irregular personal life – she married three times and had many other relationships. Henry Irving, by contrast, had a forbidding appearance. His aquiline features made him the model for Count Dracula, and not everyone admired his heavily mannered style of delivery. But he must have had a kind heart – he supported his retired actresses with regular pensions, and took Terry's two illegitimate children by the Bristol architect Edward Godwin under his wing. When they were old enough they joined his theatre company.

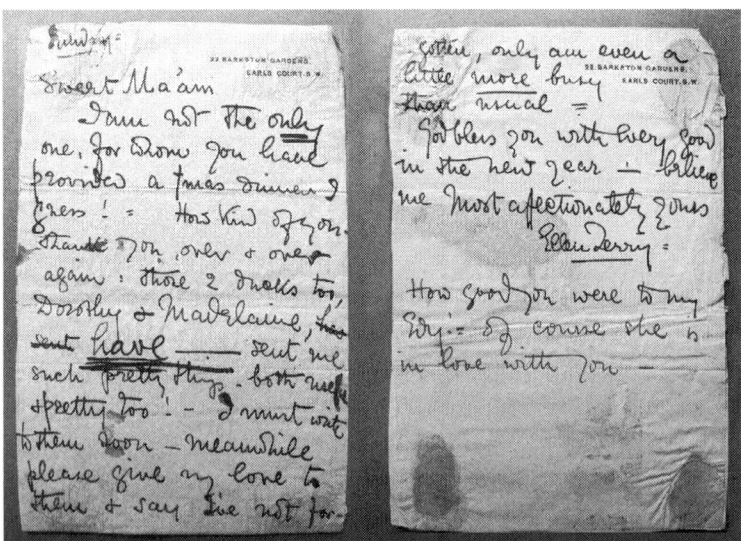

One of the few letters that escaped being sold to some foreign library for the value of its autograph, presumably because it's such a mess. (Edy is Terry's daughter)

Madeleine and Dorothy also went to many plays with 'Uncle Tom' Hardy, who loved taking them. Writing to Emma, he says:

> It was a great pleasure to take the children last night – or rather to be taken by them… it is not always one gets taken to theatres by such experienced playgoers. Their eyes were so bright, & their whisperings incessant, in their anxiety that we should not miss the points of the performance… they are such dears that it is a pleasure to go with them.

Later on he tells Emma about another outing:

> I took the girls to the theatre last night – & was more amused by their innocent talk than by the play – though they gave me some laughable specimens of slang. 'I do hope it will be something very *risqué*' said Dorothy. 'So as to make our hair curl!' – the point of it being that they wd turn round & ask me *if it was risqué* – not knowing of their own judgment.

It didn't bother Mary if a play was considered to have questionable morals. She once got into trouble with Cecil Rhodes, who went with her to see a Pinero play, *The Gay Lord Quex*. It was a light-hearted comedy about a philanderer trying to mend his ways, and as soon as it ended Rhodes had a go at Mary for having brought a young girl (probably one of her daughters) along with them to watch it. As Mary defended herself he became more and more argumentative, planting himself on a sofa in the corridor and refusing to be budged by the staff, who were trying to close the theatre. In the end they had to get the manager to come and get Rhodes out, and even then he tried to persuade Mary to follow him to his hotel 'where he promised he would finish the discussion.' It was only, she says, 'with great difficulty' that she extricated herself from this threatening proposal.

Mary may have had liberal views on the theatre; others did not. For many, the word actress was more or less synonymous with 'prostitute'. This was the view of the 'social purity' feminists who had formed the National Vigilance Association (NVA), in response to the Criminal Law Amendment Act of 1885. While the Act had the laudable effect of raising the age of consent to sixteen, and protecting children from abuse and trafficking, some of its clauses were unduly repressive. One of these was the Labouchère amendment, which made gross indecency between men illegal and caused Oscar Wilde's downfall, followed by that of countless others. But it was the clauses which criminalised brothels and soliciting that most threatened women's independence. The NVA, while considering themselves to be feminists, were staunch supporters of these measures. And Millicent Fawcett was a founder member.

The social purity movement attracted women who were determined to rid the city of anything that could be deemed 'immoral behaviour', and included temperance campaigners like Mary's aunt Louisa and her sister-in-law Maude Stanley. They were driven by religious principles and regarded the invasion of personal liberty as quite justifiable in the interests of morality. But the closing down of brothels was not high on the agenda of Sir Charles Warren, Chief Commissioner of the Metropolitan Police. He felt it to be a waste of police time, because 'as long as there is a demand for prostitutes on the part of the public there is no doubt they will exist in spite of the Vestries and Vigilance Societies, and the more they are driven out of their brothels and back slums, the worse it becomes for law and order and decency'.

So the NVA took it upon themselves to apply pressure on the police to enforce the new law. One result was that single women found it increasingly hard to find accommodation, because landlords were nervous that a house full of women might be taken for a brothel. Another was that, on the street, a woman might be accosted on suspicion of plying the evil trade on no better evidence than the fact that she was not wearing gloves, or a hat.

Mary had little time for the NVA. 'Years of work and experience have convinced me that those who begin with religion begin at the wrong end,' she wrote, going on to scold her evangelical sisters: 'Nothing can be more stern and cruel than the judgement meted out by those whose immunity from want and temptation should have made them tender to others who have fallen by the way.' She didn't believe that the Criminal Amendment Act would eradicate prostitution – 'We cannot make people good by Act of Parliament,' she said.

To social purity adherents, the theatre was more or less akin to a brothel. For a start, actresses were often inadequately clothed. Worse than that, the well-heeled theatrical clientele attracted swarms of the better class of prostitutes, who would hang about at the theatre exits in the hopes of picking up trade. In the interests of protecting children from this toxic environment, Millicent Fawcett launched a campaign to ban any child under the age of ten from working on the stage. Mary was quick to take up her pen in dissent.

This was not the only area in which Mary disagreed with Millicent, who was something of a hardliner – she was also opposed to free education and free school meals (two ideals that were close to Mary's heart) on the grounds that these would merely encourage feckless parenting. Mary's article 'Children in Theatres' in the *English Illustrated Magazine* was addressed directly at Millicent, and objected to a ban on child actors on economic grounds. 'Those who know the hard lives of the working poor', she wrote, meaning herself, 'are very indignant that a crusade should be preached against an employment which, if not abused and overdone, helps to ease the struggle for existence.'

She knew many of the families of child actors who lived in the slums which bordered theatreland, in the parish of St Giles (appropriately enough, the patron saint of lepers, beggars and cripples). A high proportion of these households had no adult male wage-earner. Mary knew one single mother who earned a pittance making linings for gentlemen's hats. Her daughter danced in the ballet at the Empire Theatre, providing a regular income for the mother and her blind son. Another, a widow with seven children in Great St Andrew's Street, depended entirely on her boy's theatre wages of ten shillings a week. Mary hardly needed to add that removing this source of income might drive those struggling women into the oldest profession.

She set out to destroy Millicent's arguments, wielding her superior knowledge like a wrecking ball:

> Mrs Fawcett can never have been behind the scenes… She writes like most people who know very little of the management of a theatre, as if 'behind the scenes' was a place where every excess, and orgie, was committed, and where everyone was allowed to do just as they pleased, without any sort of restraint, or control. There is no place, except perhaps in barracks, where such absolute obedience is enforced.

Mary maintained that the lack of space backstage made discipline essential, and as for loose morals, in eleven years' experience she had only ever come across two 'fallen' women who had been on the stage. (Presumably this did not include her friend Ellen Terry, whose chequered past somehow managed to be discounted.) Another objection to allowing children on the stage was that the work would keep them up long past their bedtime. But this argument was predicated on them having a nice clean bed waiting for them at home. Mary said that if the people who believed this 'would only come with me any night into parts of London not a mile from comfortable West End homes, I could show them streets after streets crowded with children till long after ten o'clock at night.' Again, she is talking about the parish of St Giles where children were glad of anything that delayed their return to damp homes, and beds which swarmed with vermin.

As it turned out, Millicent's campaign to ban children from the stage was very unpopular with the Victorian public. The cult of the child was at its peak – John Millais' sugary portrait of his grandson, entitled Bubbles, had been adopted as the icon of Pears soap, while the Drury Lane Theatre employed more than 150 children at a time in its pantomimes, and D'Oyly Carte were staging Gilbert and Sullivan operettas with child-only casts. The appetite for child prodigies and performers was insatiable, the sentimental adulation of them extreme. In the end the Children's Charter of 1889 did not ban child actors from the stage, though it did introduce licensing laws for theatrical managers, and forbade any child under the age of seven to work in the theatre. More importantly, it allowed the state to intervene in the family sphere if a child was at risk of abuse. It may fairly be said that both sides were happy with the outcome, and in any case Mary Jeune and Millicent Fawcett soon overcame their differences, united by a common foe in the shape of the anti-suffrage movement.

In June of 1889, *Nineteenth Century* magazine published an 'Appeal against Women's Suffrage', with more than a hundred signatories. The author of the 'Appeal' was Mary Ward, or Mrs Humphry Ward as she preferred to be known. She was one of a curious crew of campaigners for female education who were particularly averse to giving women the vote. Married to a progressive Oxford don, she had launched a programme of lectures for women to help them achieve university entrance, and it was she who suggested Somerville as the name for a new women's college, in honour of Mary Somerville, the Scottish 'Queen of Science.' When Mrs Ward and her husband first moved to London in 1881 she became interested in politics through the many new friends she made – funnily enough, 'in that happy meeting-ground of men and causes – Mrs Jeune's drawing room.' But she did not think, as a woman, that an interest in politics should extend to active involvement.

The signatories of the 'Appeal against Women's Suffrage' were an eminent lot. Heading the list was Mary's mother-in-law Lady

Stanley, redoubtable founder of Girton College. Another was Lucy Cavendish, whose name would later be given to the post-graduate Cambridge college. She took up the cause of female education after her husband Lord Frederick was murdered by the Fenians in Phoenix Park. Then there was Mrs Lynn Linton, who after separating from her husband led an independent life and found success as the writer of many anti-feminist novels. A more surprising signatory was Beatrice Potter, who later, as Beatrice Webb, changed her mind and became a suffragist.

Mary referred to the supporters of the Appeal as the 'Churchill lot,' because they included the Duchess of Marlborough (Randolph Churchill's mother), Lady Tweedmouth (Randolph's sister), Jennie Jerome (Randolph's wife)… 'and the rest of the Churchill family.' Other famous anti-suffragists include: Edith Nesbit, a Fabian, who feared that widening suffrage would merely increase the number of conservative voters. Eleanor Marx, who thought female suffrage was a bourgeois plot. Gertrude Bell, who was so powerful she didn't need a vote, and didn't see why any other women should have it.

Frank Harris was quick to offer the pages of his *Fortnightly Review* for a counter declaration which was headed by Millicent Fawcett, Elizabeth Garrett Anderson, and Emily Davies, one of Lady Stanley's co-founders at Girton. The pro-suffrage petition attracted so many signatories that they could not all be printed in the magazine, so it was decided to form a committee to choose those they considered to be most representative, grouping them under such headings as Educationists, Wives of Clergymen, Registered Medical Practitioners, Social and Philanthropic Workers, and Women Engaged in Business. Mary was invited to be on the committee, but she was less than impressed by their attempts at making the list representative:

> A meeting took place at Mrs Fawcett's house in Gower Street, at which there was a great difference of opinion as to the names to be selected, and some of the ladies on the committee had strong

personal feelings on the subject. Mrs Fawcett showed the utmost impartiality, and... the names were read out one by one... There was a good deal of hesitation and protest at first, some objecting to a peeress signing, for no reason except that she was a peeress. Another lady, well known in dramatic circles, was objected to on the ground that her character was indifferent. My remark that the list was supposed to be representative was passed over in silence, and her name was erased... At last the name of a lady... who had been one of the first pioneers of the woman's movement and one of the warmest supporters, was mentioned, only to be keenly opposed by some of the members of our committee. We who represented the moderates protested, and I asked for the reason of this rejection, on which one of the ladies of the committee said, 'It is because she is an odious woman, and I hate her!' which seemed to settle the matter.

After the 'Appeal' the anti-suffrage movement gained popularity for quite a while among people (many of them women) who liked to denounce suffragists for their sexual deviance, hysteria, lack of femininity, and general unnaturalness. Mary sadly commented that 'though logically, perhaps, the refusal to give them the Parliamentary franchise is indefensible, it seems doubtful whether the majority of women in this country are very anxious to acquire it.'

It wasn't as though women had *never* had any experience of voting. Those who were ratepayers had been able to vote in local elections on and off since the Reform Act of 1832. But in 1872 married women were again stripped of a voice. Mary as a widow could still vote, and although she remarried in 1881, she somehow escaped detection until ten years later, when she was summoned to the Courthouse in Marylebone Lane. The *Morning Post* reported on the process:

> Lady Susan Elizabeth Mary Jeune, wife of the Hon. Sir Francis Henry Jeune, was on the list as a county elector in respect of

successive occupation of 37, Wimpole Street, and 79, Harley Street. She was objected to by the Liberal agent on the ground that she was a married woman, and thereby not entitled to a vote. The Revising Barrister struck out her name.

The Real Lady Bracknell?

In which Mary collaborates with Oscar Wilde and inspires some of his best lines

T he most notable, and in my view the most tragic, omission from *Memories of Fifty Years* is that of Oscar Wilde. It is no surprise that his name is absent from my great-great-grandmother's memoir, since it could hardly be whispered in public for years after his downfall, and it was not until the 21st century that it became not only acceptable but fashionable to choose it for your child.

It is not possible to prove that Mary was the model for Wilde's most famous character, the formidable matriarch of *The Importance of Being Earnest*. But I was delighted to come across the notion in a book called *Marylebone Lives – Rogues, Romantics and Rebels*, a collection of stories about various characters who lived in the Marylebone area of London. In a section entitled 'Mad, Bad and Dangerous to Know', *Marylebone Journal* contributor Tom Hughes had written a chapter entitled: 'Lady Mary Jeune, the real Lady Bracknell', in which he suggests that she was the source of Wilde's inspiration. It was but a short step from this to discovering that Oscar was not only inspired by Mary, he was actually friends with her for many years; something I don't believe my family were aware of – or if they were, they never mentioned it.

In 1885, at the age of 40, Mary launched a journalistic career that within seven years would see her name emblazoned in news media around the globe. She started out modestly enough, with a pair of articles on the 'rescue work' she'd been engaged in for a number of years. Bearing the quintessentially Victorian titles 'Helping the

Fallen' and 'Saving the Innocent', they appeared in the *Fortnightly Review*, a high-quality journal whose mission statement was to publish the 'unbiased expression of many and various minds on Politics, Literature, Philosophy, Science, and Art'. Already we can see in Mary's writing her trademark tone of unquestionable authority, and a tendency to sound disapproving. Not of the fallen women she had dealings with, but of 'the richer women in our country… for the little care and interest they show in their servants' – for most of her prospects had been in domestic service before their 'fall' cost them their livelihood. Mary was no socialist, but her castigation of the well-heeled was to be an underlying theme in almost everything she wrote subsequently, whether it was about poverty, the New Woman, or even the society of which she was a key member.

There followed a gap of two years before anything else appeared in print. Meanwhile, one May afternoon, Oscar Wilde came to call. He had just taken on the job of editing a 'vulgar and trivial' (his words) woman's magazine called *The Lady's World*. Oscar now had a wife and two children to support, and so needed a regular income. At the same time the magazine's publishers, Cassell & Co, were struggling amidst an explosion of publications aimed at the growing market of middle class women who could afford to buy them. Their idea was that Oscar's celebrity status would entice a wider readership.

Women's periodicals of the time generally confined themselves to fashion and domestic concerns, but Oscar had loftier ambitions. He wanted to produce a magazine that dealt 'not merely with what women wear, but what they think.' In fact it was to be a flagship of proto-feminism, with pieces by 'women of intellect, culture and position'. It was with this in mind that he came to see Mary, for she knew just about everyone there was to know in all three categories. And so it was that he ensconced himself in her Harley Street drawing room for a whole afternoon, while together they pored over her compendious address book. It yielded quite a few titled persons and even a princess, all good for sales. The next day

Oscar happily reported to his publishers that 'Mrs Jeune was very delighted with the idea of our project', and he threw himself into it with enthusiasm.

Mary and Oscar had known and admired each other for a long time before either of them had work published. Oscar moved to London in 1878, the year that Johnny Stanley died. He came with little in the way of connections, but was lucky enough to share a house just off the Strand with the artist Frank Miles, who had plenty. Miles had already established himself as a society darling with his drawings of 'professional beauties' in *Life* magazine, of which he was artist-in-chief. Ladies from the upper echelons of society came flocking to the ramshackle studio apartment that Miles shared with Oscar, to commission his pencil portraits. Oscar, freshly down from Oxford and hoping to become a society darling himself, wore his scholarship lightly and his flamboyant outfits earnestly. Through Miles Oscar got to know Lord Ronald Leveson-Gower, who would have been a pivotal figure in the gay scene if such a thing had existed at the time, and his sister Constance, Duchess of Westminster: a 'most fascinating, Circe-like, brilliant woman', said Oscar. Lord Ronald, who is thought to be the model for Lord Henry Wotton in *The Picture of Dorian Grey*, was renowned as a 'sodomite' and had already been obliged to sue the journal *Man of the World* for allegations about his sexuality, but it was not hard to come out on top with money and a title behind you. Constance and Ronald were Mary's cousins by marriage, so it is quite possibly through them that she and Oscar originally became acquainted. She often visited Grosvenor House where Constance lived with her husband the Duke of Westminster, the richest man in London. Given his wealth, Mary found his household arrangements 'curiously economical' – she was impressed by the enormous quantities of fruit placed on the buffet, but apparently 'it was all made of wax, as Lord Westminster thought it an extravagance to have real fruit!'

Mary at that time was holding what she called 'five o'clocks' at Wimpole Street – the recent loss of her first husband doesn't seem to have dampened her enthusiasm for entertaining. Oscar and Frank thought these were brilliant, inspiring them to start their own parties, which they called 'Tea and Beauties'. The only letter from Oscar to Mary that has survived dates from this period.

> Dear Mrs Stanley,
> The fates are always against me! And on the night when the only place in London worth going to is your brilliant salon I find myself so engaged that I cannot escape. Still, if you will allow me I will try and come. Who would not "venture for such merchandise"?
> Believe me, truly yours, Oscar Wilde.

Later he would reminisce: 'There were three inevitables – death, quarter-day, and Lady Jeune's parties'.

Now, seven years on, work began on elevating *The Ladies' World* into a quality magazine. After his meeting with Mary Oscar fired off countless letters to prospective contributors, promising payment of a guinea a page. At the same time the word 'lady' was going to have to be removed from the title, as it met with 'the strongest opposition' from some of the women writers he approached. It took nearly six months of negotiation to persuade Cassell's to accept a new title, but eventually they did and in November 1887 *The Woman's World* burst onto newsagents' shelves. Fashion was not disregarded but moved to the back pages, giving way to more serious articles such as 'The Position of Woman', 'Oxford Ladies' Colleges', and 'The Children of a Great City' (a report on child poverty by Mary Jeune). The new magazine was a great success, the first edition selling out in hours. 'Mr Oscar Wilde has triumphed,' said the Nottingham Evening Post.

The following year saw Mary's output grow, with three articles in the *National Review* (edited by Alfred Austin, later to become one of the least talented poet laureates in history), and a piece on the Brahan Seer in *Murray's Magazine*. Oscar commissioned her to write a report on the Irish Industrial Art exhibition at Olympia. The central attraction was a fake Donegal village peopled with real Irish craftswomen weaving, knitting and making lace. Mary was enthusiastic about the Irish revival of traditional crafts, and noted that the English would do well to follow their example by providing state-subsidised technical training for women. In her article she chastises England for losing the butter-making contest in Manchester to an Irish agricultural college. Oscar regularly commissioned articles on Irish culture, *The Woman's World* providing him with a platform to showcase his homeland, and make up for the marginalisation he often experienced as an Irishman in Society.

By the same token, titled contributors bolstered his social status. The first thing he'd done after combing through Mary's address book was to draft a letter to Princess Christian, one of Queen Victoria's less favourite daughters. As Mary was on friendly terms with her, she was to deliver it for him. It was perhaps the princess' own ill health and related opium addiction that inspired her to champion nurses' rights and education, and to found both the British Nurses' Association and the British Red Cross. Her piece on 'Nursing as a Profession for Women' was published in *The Woman's World* the following year.

Oscar was a keen supporter of rights for women, whether titled or untitled, and the magazine ran many articles on women's work and education. There was some fiction – Olive Schreiner contributed a short story – and not too much politics. He invited Millicent Fawcett to contribute an article on female suffrage, then took issue with her in his Literary Notes column because she 'deprecates the engagement of ladies of education as dressmakers and milliners'. Oscar's opinion was that dressmaking should be seen 'not merely as a learned profession, but as a fine art.'

The success of *The Woman's World* was short-lived. Oscar

didn't see eye-to-eye with his publishers, who complained that the magazine was too literary. Besides, they had a strict no-smoking policy, which made the office environment unappealing. His hours there became shorter and shorter, and in less than two years *The Woman's World* folded. It didn't really matter to Oscar because he was beginning to make a success at his writing, with *The Happy Prince and other Tales*, *The Picture of Dorian Gray* and *The Soul of Man Under Socialism*. At lunch at Mary's he recounted with delight how the *St James Gazette* had condemned *Dorian Gray* as improper, causing it to sell like wildfire.

At the same time, Mary's journalistic horizons were expanding. She was still writing essays on urban deprivation, but now ventured into more contentious areas. These included a sceptical account of the newly nascent New Woman, and, more bizarrely, a broadside at General Booth, founder of the Salvation Army. Booth was already a controversial figure and Mary seemed keen to stoke the controversy, using sarcasm as her weapon of choice and the provocative title 'Anti-Humbug' – though when this was later reprinted in a collection of her essays, it had been watered down to a more anodyne 'The Salvation Army'.

In 1991 Francis Jeune was appointed President of the Probate, Divorce and Admiralty Division, and knighted. In simple English, he was Britain's chief divorce judge. Mary was now Lady Jeune, and regarded as THE leader of London Society. No-one thought her prestige was due to her husband's promotion, by the way, rather the opposite. The *Manchester Daily Dispatch* made no bones about it: 'Her husband would never have been a judge but for her', they said. Mary herself was under no delusions about this. 'With a bright wife and plenty of money,' she wrote, 'a man may attain to any social position. His appearance, his past, his capacity, all are immaterial if his wife knows how to play her cards.'

Their new status was celebrated with a move, from Wimpole to Harley Street. This wasn't exactly radical, as the new house lay exactly at the back of the old one, and they only had to cart their goods across Wimpole Mews, which lay in between. But the new house was slightly bigger, in order, presumably, to accommodate the ever expanding 'crushes' rather than a growing family.

Invitations to Mary's functions were now considered essential for anyone who wanted to get on. 'Fortunate were those', wrote William H. Rideing, 'who, visiting London, took with them a letter of introduction to Lady Jeune'. Rideing was the managing editor of *North American Review*, the transatlantic equivalent of the *Fortnightly Review* – i.e. a non-partisan publication that didn't shrink from handling controversial questions. Fortunate indeed was Rideing, on gaining entry to Mary's entourage. He was completely bowled over by his hostess, gushing lyrically:

> A girl in figure, simply dressed, and fresh as her own heather, with large and beautiful eyes, which might be likened to one of her native lochs in their changing moods, now full, cool, and placid, as in calm and shadow, then as a loch swept by wind and sun, luminous, shimmering and dancing with, in her case, a sort of mischievous and communicative humour.

Mary Jeune was not only winsome, but clever – surely she was just the person to write an article on London Society for the *North American Review*.

Mary's article appeared in Rideing's journal in May of 1892, and instantly kicked up a storm. It was not what he, or anyone else, was expecting. The article was highly critical! Apparently the very fabric of British Society was under threat: 'When all that is needed to insure an entrance into the highest society in England is unlimited wealth,' she pronounced, 'is it to be wondered at that the deterioration which is going on is much more complete, and will be more disastrous in its effects, than any one likes to admit?' And who was to blame for this deterioration? Why, it was 'only the outcome and logical result of the easy-going manner in which women of the highest rank and culture have allowed the old-fashioned rules and restraints which governed society to be relaxed.' Again, it was women of the leisured classes who got the sharp edge of Mary's pen.

Reactions to the publication of her piece were immediate, and widespread. If Mary had been an object of interest to the news media before, it was nothing compared to the feeding frenzy thrown up by 'London Society'. In the year that followed its publication, Mary Jeune's name was mentioned no less than 2000 times in the press, and her essays were in great demand, commanding a reward of as much as £10 – equivalent to something like £1000 today. The 'London Society' article was reported as far afield as the *Petersburg Times* of Australia who said

> Lady Jeune is at the present time perhaps the most interesting feminine personality in London society. Probably no other woman has so many friends and has accomplished so much good, solid work. On the other hand, she is par excellence a fashionable hostess, and many were scandalized at her late attacks on the smart world, of which she forms so integral a part.

Meanwhile the London correspondent of the *New York Times* agreed with Mary:

> One who has watched what calls itself society here with observant eyes for any length of time cannot but rejoice that a serious and brave little woman has been impelled to give voice to the disgust which the spectacle inspires in honest people.

Other reactions, however, were far from positive. It was the tone of the piece as much as its contents that upset readers. W. H. Mallock, author of satirical novels and controversial religious works, submitted twelve pages of critique to the *North American Review*, mildly remarking: 'Though her details were right the effect of the whole was wrong.' A far stronger tone was taken by Lady

Florence Balfour, aristocratic president of the London Society of Women's Suffrage. She was furious that Mary should wash her country's dirty linen in front of the American public. The very next edition of *North American Review* printed her rebuttal:

> Lady Jeune in her painting uses a large canvas, her assertions are drawn in much bold and sweeping lines, her colours are so coarse, her subject is so glaringly unlike nature, and her execution is so masterly in its technique, that it is permissible to admire for a minute before turning to the duty of contradicting these assertions, toning down these colours, representing the subject as it really exists and varnishing the whole with a thin coating of accuracy.

Confidently headed 'A Last Word on London Society', Lady Balfour's article was nothing of the sort. Mary wrote at least three more essays on the subject, and in none of them did she backtrack in the slightest.

If many were shocked or upset by her criticisms, others must have been amused by her melodramatic figures of speech. For example:

> Luxury, ease, comfort, are the watchwords of a large part of society in London, and they are undermining our society as surely and as certainly as they did that of ancient Rome.

W.H. Mallock took issue with this statement, pointing out that

> ...when an aristocracy falls after it has grown corrupt and luxurious, its fall is due, not to its corruption, but to some common cause which has produced both. The French Revolution was due not to bad morals but to bad farming...

All this was a gift to Oscar, who had once confessed: 'Of course I plagiarise, it is the privilege of the appreciative man.' And so, in the famous handbag scene, Lady Bracknell complains of 'a contempt for the ordinary decencies of family life that reminds one of the worst excesses of the French Revolution.'

This is what Tom Hughes has to say about Mary's 'London Society' article:

> To be sure, there's a touch of the rantings of Lady Bracknell in all this earnestness. Wilde's character, almost certainly inspired by Lady Jeune, bangs on about the decay of good society…

Once this notion has been sown in the mind it's impossible not to hear the voice of Lady B. in many of Mary's pronouncements. The young woman in 'London Society' whose life is 'one round of pleasure from morning to night' sounds remarkably like an acquaintance of Lady Bracknell's: 'I had some crumpets with Lady Harbury, who seems to me to be living entirely for pleasure now.' And years later, long after Oscar's downfall, Mary was interviewed in *Strand* magazine, the *Hello!* of the Victorian age. At some point she states: 'Twenty five years ago a woman had no opinions until she was married.' Pure Wilde…

There can be no doubt that Oscar read Mary's essays, as they are referenced in *The Green Carnation*, Robert Hichens best-selling satire on Wilde and his milieu. Hichens was introduced into Oscar's circle by Bosie (Lord Alfred Douglas), and he must have taken notes because he recycled many of their conversations verbatim for his book. In it, Oscar is thinly disguised as Esme Amarinth, while Bosie is Lord Reggie. In this scene they are discussing the London literary scene with their hostess Mrs Windsor. She starts the conversation by talking about Eliza Lynn Lynton, the well-known anti-feminist journalist:

> 'Mrs Linton's articles are really getting so very noisy. Don't you think they rather suggest Bedlam?'

'To me they suggest nothing whatever,' said Amarinth wearily. 'I cannot distinguish one from another. They are all like sheep that have gone astray.'

'I must say I prefer them to Lady Jeune's,' said Mrs Windsor.

'Lady Jeune catches society by the throat and worries it,' said Madame Valets.

'She worries it very inartistically,' added Lord Reggie.

'Ah!' said Amarinth, as the ladies rose to go into the drawing-room; 'she makes one great mistake. She judges of Society by her own parties, and looks at life through the spectacles of a divorce court judge. No wonder she is the bull terrier of modern London life.'

By this time Mary had certainly acquired a fearsome reputation. An American paper said that her guests must now be 'secretly afraid of their clever hostess' trenchant pen', and those who had never met her may indeed have imagined her to be a bull terrier, or a gorgon. In the flesh, however, she was anything but. Oscar took Bosie to meet Mary at Harley Street – he thought her 'as bright as a butterfly', and on his return to Oxford wrote about her in the undergraduate journal he edited, *The Spirit Lamp*:

> Of the literary ladies who are exceptions to the rule that 'Women who write' are in strict accord with their writings, only two instances occur at this moment. These are Lady Jeune and Mrs Mona Caird, who are among the most charming women of our acquaintance. To read Lady Jeune, you would think her severe and puritanic in the extreme, embodiment of the spirit of all the Covenanters. She is the very opposite...'

In some ways it is a shame that Edith Evans' iconic portrayal of Lady Bracknell has fossilised her in the public imagination as more or less terrifying. It is worth noting that subsequent actors have preferred to interpret her as more approachable, while remaining, naturally, 'a complete stranger to self-doubt' (Una Stubbs). In 2004 Wendy Craig had this to say: 'As soon as I read the play, I knew exactly how I wanted to play her. She didn't strike me as a downbeat, sour lady, but as a sprightly, flirtatious 50-year-old. I tried to make her charming, urbane and attractive.'

As to what Mary thought of Oscar, there's very little to go on apart from the 'so delightfully clever, so brilliant!' with which she first introduced him to Frank Harris. But William H. Rideing visited the Jeunes shortly after Oscar's downfall. 'Let me recall a house in Harley Street,' he says coyly, 'I will call the hostess Lady B—.' Although he took great pains to conceal everyone's identities, it is pretty clear who he is talking about:

> …talk again turned to the 'brilliant and erratic man who had come to grief in a recent scandal.'
>
> With a sly look from her husband to me, she said, 'He was so nice, and isn't it a pity? But I dare say that the next time you come to England you'll find him here again.'
>
> 'Never!' cried her husband, who was one of the most distinguished of English judges. 'I' – with extreme emphasis on the pronoun – 'I draw the line at those who have been in jail.'
>
> 'Oh, don't be so narrow, dear,' she protested. 'They are the most interesting people in the world.'

Two sides of the Irish Question

In which Mary keeps a foot firmly in both camps, and does what she can to find an answer

There is perhaps no question apart from 'Is there a God?' which has lasted as long as the Irish one without getting a satisfactory answer. A thorough overview would fill several volumes, but I will attempt to put it in a nutshell. The Irish people began to feel resentment towards the English as long ago as 1171, when King Henry II invaded Ireland. But the Question became far more thorny as the 18th century turned into the 19th, and the British government, having crushed the Irish Rebellion of 1798, brought in the Acts of Union which made Ireland part of the United Kingdom. Ninety percent of the land was owned by 'Anglo-Irish' landlords, many of whom did not even live there. Then the British Government's failure to act during the Great Famine, which saw the population nearly halved through death and migration, gave birth to the Fenians and an even stronger hunger for independence.

By the time Mary came on the scene, British politics were dominated by the question of Home Rule for Ireland. It divided London society and the Liberal Party, and destroyed Gladstone. It also had a very bad effect on the health of the main contenders. Mary never expressed a preference for either side, but admitted to feeling a 'deep excitement' about this issue, which bisected the British nation like a knife. If it added spice to her gatherings, that was no problem – she determinedly kept close friends on both sides of the argument. And at some point it seems that she became an incognito go-between for the opposing factions.

Mary's sympathy for the nationalist cause was no doubt spurred by her friendship with the Irish journalist Justin McCarthy, whom she first met at Lady Waldegrave's in her early days in London. At that time he was editor of the *Morning Star*, a radical pro-peace newspaper, but later he became Britain's first Home Rule MP. He had for a long time been good friends with Mary's mother-in-law Henrietta Stanley, but as she was fiercely opposed to Home Rule, when McCarthy got elected his relations with her became 'somewhat disturbed', as he delicately put it. By the time this happened though, he had formed a firm bond with Mary, for he wrote:

> I owe to Lady Stanley of Alderley one friendship, for it is indeed a friendship, which has lasted during many years, and is I hope destined to last many years longer – the friendship of Mrs Stanley, as she then was... and now Lady Jeune.

Before he became a nationalist MP this quiet intellectual had been the darling of London Society. Suddenly, according to T.P. O'Connor, editor of the *Star* newspaper, he was ostracised by all his old friends – 'with the honourable exception' however, 'of Mrs Jeune'. In fashionable drawing rooms women physically drew away from him, as though he were contaminated. But Mary remained faithful. She had always liked McCarthy, and in her opinion he was 'entirely unfitted to be a member of the Home Rule party. Cultivated, accomplished, gentle by nature... he was much happier when absorbed in his books and writings.'

T.P. O'Connor was another person who Mary's more conventional friends were shocked to see in her drawing-room. After one of her parties, the effete poet Coventry Patmore wrote to a friend:

> The assembly was mainly Conservative, but all parties were represented. For example (don't faint) I was introduced to T. P. O'Connor, the great Parnellite!

O'Connor was another Home Rule MP, with the unique distinction of holding an English seat (Liverpool) for nearly fifty years. He also founded and edited the *Star* and the *Sun*, newspapers that quickly acquired enormous circulations by focusing on the problems of the underprivileged. O'Connor was a life-long snuff-taker, and generally known as Tay Pay in mockery of his Irish accent.

He became notorious for sparking a riot in the House of Commons when the second Home Rule Bill was being presented. Joseph Chamberlain, formerly a radical Liberal, had taken up an anti-Home Rule stance and helped to engineer the fatal split in the Liberal Party. During a members' sitting Tay Pay referred to him as Judas Chamberlain, and his nationalist followers took up a cry of 'Judas! Judas!'. A wild free-for-all ensued, the likes of which had never been seen in the House before, with a struggling, cursing mass of MPs filling the space between the front benches. Within five minutes or so the Speaker managed to restore order, begging members to allow this 'regrettable incident to pass into oblivion' – which of course it didn't. O'Connor apologised for his use of language, stayed the course, and ended up as Father of the House.

Mary's sympathies with the Irish cause were known if not exactly accepted by her Conservative friends. Justin McCarthy relates an incident that took place shortly after Mary's husband Johnny died, when she invited him to dinner. There was a good handful of Tories round the table, including Randolph Churchill and Arthur Balfour. Randolph, who loved a wind-up, insisted in 'his cheery boyish way' that Mary sing a rebel song, *The Wearing of the Green*, in honour, he said, of McCarthy's nationalist leanings. Mary was more than happy to comply and sang the song 'with great sweetness and spirit', says McCarthy. (One of the many mysteries about her is how she managed to acquire such an impressive repertoire of protest songs.) *The Wearing of the Green* dates from the 1798 Rebellion, and has as its refrain:

> St Patrick's Day no more we'll keep, his colours can't be seen
> For they're hanging men and women for the wearing of the green

Balfour, it seems, was immune to these poignant sentiments, however sweetly sung. Later he would become Chief Secretary of Ireland, where his ruthless suppression of unrest won him the nickname Bloody Balfour.

Balfour was not a particular friend of Mary's, but an earlier chief secretary, William Forster, was, and she devotes several pages to him in her memoir. Forster earned himself a similar, if less alliterative, nickname for his part in suppressing Irish agitation – he was known as Buckshot Forster. However he was very conflicted over the Irish Question. Raised a Quaker, Forster had visited Connemara on a relief mission during the famine, and had been deeply affected by what he saw there. During his tenure police were using battering rams to evict tenants who couldn't pay the rent, and burning down their homes. Forster tried to introduce a bill to award compensation to the victims of evictions, but it was thrown out by the Lords. Of course this only intensified agrarian unrest. In order to try and contain the violence Forster felt obliged to bring in a law which allowed for internment without trial: this he described as the most painful duty he had ever had to perform.

The immediate result of Forster's Coercion Act was many attempts on his life, which he enjoyed describing to Mary, for he plainly had a well-developed sense of humour. She describes how he read her a letter he'd received from an Irishman who wanted to kill him:

> The writer began his letter by applying all the opprobrious epithets with which the Irish used to speak of Mr. Forster, and then went on to say he had waited in the Phoenix Park for many days to assassinate him, which, however, he had been prevented from doing by the sight of his [Forster's] beautiful niece who always walked with her uncle…giving as his reason that he had not the heart to disturb the peace of so young and beautiful a creature by this vile crime. He wound up the letter by saying Mr

Forster must not always expect that to act a deterrent, as, to use his own words, 'he had sent all these tender fancies to hell.' Mr Forster read this letter with great delight, and chuckled over it.

Forster had many narrow escapes which could be regarded as nothing less than miraculous – his successor, Lord Frederick Cavendish, held office for only one week before being murdered in the Phoenix park, together with his undersecretary Thomas Burke.

Mary was – unwittingly – to put Forster's sense of humour to the test. Standing in opposition to him in Parliament was Charles Stewart Parnell, the leader of the Home Rule Party. Although he was revered by Irish Nationalists as 'Ireland's Uncrowned King', Parnell was a surprising contender for the title. He was a Protestant landlord who spoke with an English accent, and was largely ignorant of Irish history. His hostility to Britain seems to have been inspired by an unhappy childhood spent in English boarding schools. Mary had met him through Justin McCarthy, and Parnell was clearly taken with her, because he insisted on coming to visit her at home one Sunday afternoon – a day when Forster was also likely to pay a call.

On the day of Parnell's appointment Mary took appropriate precautions.

> Knowing that Mr Forster might possibly arrive during his visit, and that their relations were rather strained, I told my parlourmaid (a most confidential person) that she was not to admit anyone while Mr Parnell was upstairs. Unfortunately, Mr Parnell arrived rather later than I expected, and was admitted, while Mr Forster, who came almost simultaneously, and saw Mr Parnell enter my house, was told I was not at home!

One can only admire Mary's capacity for understatement in describing their relations as 'rather strained' – Forster was viewed as no less than a monster by the Nationalists. He wasn't upset by being turned away at the door, but afterwards whenever he saw Mary he would tease her about the near-miss. It wasn't long before Parnell was imprisoned in Kilmainham Gaol, for supporting the No Rent Manifesto, and when he was released the following year Forster resigned from his post. The Irish Question had not been good for his health – in fact he used to say that Ireland had killed him.

A couple of months before he died, in January 1886, he wrote Mary a long letter about the still-unsolved Irish Question. He asked her to keep it from the press, and although she included the text in her memoir she discreetly blanked out all the names. 'Of this I am sure,' he told her, 'it will be far better to make Parnell the legal Governor of Ireland, than to leave him as he is, its illegitimate ruler.'

As Forster's health declined, Mary wrote to him to tell him that one of the Irish members of Parliament often inquired kindly after him. He wrote back: 'I am pleased at what you tell me, if they could only see poor Buckshot now they would be sorry for him, I think.' He died the night before the first Home Rule Bill was presented.

Parnell was brought down in the end not by his political rivals, but by his long-term relationship with a married upper-class English woman, Katherine O'Shea, who bore him three children. Her husband refused to divorce her, possibly because she was expecting a handsome inheritance from an aunt. When news of the affair broke Parnell lost many of his Catholic supporters because they could not condone adultery, and his health took a downward dive. He did marry Katie in the end, but after only four months he died in her arms, a tragic end to a brilliant career.

When Katie's aunt died her will was immediately contested by the rest of the family, and it so happened that the judge presiding over the case was none other than Francis Jeune. Mary scurried to the courtroom, a thing she rarely did as Francis did not like women (even his own wife) attending unless they were witnesses. But the case was settled out of court: 'a disappointment to those [she means herself] who had looked forward to a long and interesting controversy.' Katie's detractors – and she had many – called her Kitty, a slang term for a woman of loose morals. Mary, however, only ever refers to her respectfully as 'Mrs Parnell'.

Another, milder, casualty of the Irish question was John Bright, MP for Birmingham, a Quaker and radical reformer. He had made important contributions to Gladstone's Landlord and Tenant Act of 1870, the first land act to address the interests of the tenants rather than the landlords. But he would not support the Home Rule Bill, and because he commanded great respect in the Liberal party he was seen to have done more damage to it than any other individual. He spent many hours at Mary's house shedding bitter tears, rather like the Walrus and the Carpenter, at having to vote against his own party. He told her that at the House of Commons he would sit in the library until the division bell rang, as he could not bear to 'be cheered by a party [i.e. the Tories] who were antipathetic to him in every sense of the word'. He never met Gladstone face to face again.

The Home Rule Bill was disastrous for Gladstone – it split the Liberal party in two and lost him the 1886 general election. Those who opposed it feared that it would lead to independence for Ireland, and they were not wrong. But something needed to be done about the unrest that was getting out of hand. A series of Coercion Bills – roughly one a year since the 1801 Act of Union – had notably failed to quell the populace, in fact if anything had spurred them on to greater struggle. In 1885 the Lord Lieutenant of Ireland (equivalent of a monarch or viceroy) was Lord Carnarvon, a Liberal peer who had turned Conservative. His idea was that a solution might be 'some such arrangement as existed in the English colonies', and with that in mind he proposed meeting with Parnell to discuss options.

The idea of negotiating with Parnell would have been viewed with absolute horror by most of his government, so the meeting was set up in great secrecy – only two of his colleagues knew about it. Great efforts were made to hide it from public knowledge. The crowned and the uncrowned 'kings' met in an uninhabited house in London, in a very unregal room full of furniture draped in dust sheets. It had to be in a place where there were no servants who might overhear something and leak it to the press. And who was involved in setting up this meeting of arch enemies? None other than Mary, apparently, although it wasn't until 1925 that T.P. O'Connor spilled the beans to the *Irish Independent*.

> **Arranged Historic Interview**
> Mr T.P. O'Connor rather fancies that one of the persons who arranged the famous interview between Lord Carnarvon and Parnell was the still living, and very active, Lady St Helier.

This 'honourable confidence of two gentlemen within the four walls of that room', as Carnarvon described it, or melodramatic cloak-and-daggery, as others might, would never have become known – let alone 'famous' – if Parnell hadn't told everyone about it a year later. He claimed that all sorts of promises had been held out to him by Carnarvon, who denied everything. But, as predicted, Carnarvon's flirtation with devolution outraged the Party. It destroyed his career – he was forced to resign, and never returned to office. He died four years later, yet another victim of the Irish Question.

Of course in her memoir Mary gives no hint of her involvement in that clandestine intrigue. She makes reference only to many a delightful weekend spent with the Carnarvons at Highclere, now better known as Downton Abbey, while mildly remarking that Carnarvon's 'one aim was the pacification of Ireland.'

We can only imagine what her opinion was of her son-in-law St John Brodrick, subsequently Lord Midleton. Brodrick was a classic absentee landlord who owned more than 6000 acres at Midleton, near Cork. Although his family had owned the land for more than a century he didn't think of himself as Irish, and had a very condescending attitude towards those who were – in 1883 he caused uproar in the House of Commons by dismissing the lot of them as 'an impecunious and garrulous race'. He remained implacably opposed to Home Rule even after the Anglo-Irish Treaty of 1921. It's hard to find anything flattering to say about St John (pronounced Sinjon). The *Dictionary of Irish Biography* describes him rather neatly as having 'a sense of superiority not always justified by events'.

When he married Mary's daughter Madeleine, he was Secretary of State for War in the Conservative government under Arthur Balfour. It was the time of the second Boer War, when the British instigated concentration camps in South Africa. Overcrowding, underfeeding and bad hygiene led to the deaths of over 26,000 women and children in the camps – nevertheless Brodrick defended them in Parliament, insisting that internees were voluntary, contented, and comfortable – none of which was true. The following year Brodrick was shifted to the post of Secretary of State for India, whereupon the *Times* correspondent George Morrison wrote to his editor:

> Dear Mr Moberly Bell,
> None of us here could understand why Brodrick who displayed such singular incapacity at the War Office, should have been entrusted with the India Portfolio. I remember the man well at your table, a dull man who sat with his mouth half agape in order to assist his hearing. I remember how shocked I was to hear the light way in which he spoke of the appointment of Sir Redvers Buller to South Africa, and the stories he told of the general which chiefly bore upon his wonderful capacity for swilling champagne.

One can hardly envy Madeleine being wed to such a person, twenty years her senior and with a daughter by his first marriage almost as old as herself. But Madeleine had been languishing on the shelf for quite a while – her younger sister Dorothy had already been married for six years. No doubt the fawning press coverage

of this 'brilliant society affair' and the lavish wedding presents were some compensation. These last numbered six hundred or so, and included ornaments bejewelled with diamond, pearl, and ruby, pieces of precious silver and lace, embroidery and enamel, and a silver gilt inkstand from the King.

Also Madeleine now had access to three homes, in Ireland, London, and Surrey. Brodrick's house at Peper Harrow, near Godalming, was an imposing box-shaped manor with grounds landscaped by Capability Brown. It was here that the first rules of cricket were laid down, and, according to family lore, the last estate in Britain to boast a working man-trap. In 1913 Brodrick added a third storey to this already substantial house. After the second World War it was sold and turned into a rehabilitation centre for wayward children, who made a bold attempt to restore the house to its original state by setting fire to the upper floors. The marriage seems to have been reasonably successful, producing two sons: Francis after seven years, and Michael ten years later, when Madeleine was 44. The *Halifax Evening Courier* tactfully remarked: 'the increase in the family has been leisurely.'

St John Brodrick had a sister, Lady Albinia, who occupied the opposite end of the political spectrum to her brother, being a militant Irish Republican. The year that Brodrick and Madeleine married, she cut ties with the rest of the family and moved to Ireland. She trained as a nurse and bought a plot of land on the south coast of the Iveragh Peninsula, where she drained four acres of bog and set up an agricultural cooperative. She used her inheritance to build a hospital on the land, but was never granted a licence to run it, whether because of her politics, her sex, her nationality, or her religion (Protestant), nobody knows. It now stands as a picturesque ruin near the village of Castlecove on the Ring of Kerry.

Albinia became fluent in Irish, albeit with a posh English accent, and changed her name to Gobnait Ní Bhruadair. She was vegetarian and teetotal, cycled everywhere, and was a devoted nurse and member of Sinn Féin. When she was sixty-one she was shot in the leg by Loyalist forces whilst on a Republican errand, and arrested for refusing to stop her bicycle when ordered. Like Parnell, she was put in Kilmainham jail where she immediately went on hunger strike. After two weeks, close to death, they released her and she managed to continue her nursing and political activities into a ripe old age. I think even Mary might have regarded her as 'beyond the pale'.

Black Lives Matter

*In which Mary invites a civil rights activist
to have tea with her and the children*

One day in the spring of 1894, Mary was enjoying a peaceful afternoon at Arlington Manor, her country house in Berkshire. Randolph Churchill had just left, having been there for nearly a whole week. Randolph in a good mood had a kind of boyish charm, but in a bad one was quite impossible. He had always suffered from unpredictable mood swings – Mary mildly remarks that 'though this added greatly to the excitement of a visit he might happen to pay, it had its drawbacks...' Now however his behaviour was becoming even more erratic. Only a short time before, at one of Mary's lunch parties in London, Randolph had suddenly excused himself from the table with 'urgent business' and stalked out of the room, followed discreetly by a Mr Winn, who was Conservative Whip at the time. After a few moments Winn returned, his face 'pale as a ghost'. Mary was concerned. 'Has anything happened?' she asked. It transpired that Randolph had requested a private talk with Winn, and arranged to leave early with him for this purpose. But when Winn followed him out into the hall, Randolph suddenly turned on him, cried 'Can one never get rid of you and your talks!' and flounced out of the house.

Less than a year later he would be dead from 'general paralysis of the insane', probably caused by syphilis, though an alternative theory is that he had a brain tumour. Either way, after his visit Mary was exhausted. She told the servants that she was not 'at home' to visitors so that she could spend the rest of the day relaxing with her daughters.

Nevertheless, when the footman said there were some people

at the front door, and handed her the Mayor of Newbury's card, she got up and went to welcome them. On the doorstep stood the mayor, Mr Elliott, and at his side a smartly-dressed African American woman by the name of Ida B. Wells. Ida had just given a talk in Newbury on the escalation of lynching in the southern states of America, and the mayor had told her that she really ought to meet Lady Jeune, because she was 'one of the most influential and cultured women of the British aristocracy.' Without missing a beat, Mary invited Ida to come in and have tea with her and the children, so that she could tell her all about her anti-lynching crusade.

Ida was born into slavery and orphaned at the age of fourteen. She worked as a teacher to support her five siblings, later moving to Memphis where she attended college and started working as a journalist. At the age of 22 she foreshadowed Rosa Parks' bus protest by refusing to move from a 1st class ladies' carriage on the Chesapeake and Ohio Railroad. When the conductor pulled her by the arm, she sank her teeth into the back of his hand and he had to call on reinforcements to drag her from the carriage. She sued the railway company and won, but then had her victory overturned by the Supreme Court.

At 27 Ida became editor and co-owner of the *Memphis Free Speech and Headlight* newspaper, where she reported regularly on the lynchings of black men, women and children. In the 1890s these extrajudicial executions reached an all-time high, averaging 175 a year, and included torture, hanging, and burning alive. Some local people did not take kindly to Ida's reportage, and in 1892 an angry white mob ransacked the newspaper's offices and destroyed the printing presses. This hardened Ida's resolve to expose racial injustice, and she decided to take her cause to what she hoped would be a more receptive audience – the British public.

She was not wrong. In five months in Great Britain, at clubs and church halls in Liverpool, Manchester, Newcastle, Bristol and London, she delivered 102 lectures about the wave of lynching back home. All were well received by press and public alike, and their sympathetic response caused great shame among the American elite, who actually cared what the Brits thought of them. One immediate outcome was a boycott of the cotton trade. When English audiences expressed shock that such terrible things were allowed to happen in America, and asked why the churches did not intervene, Ida did not mince her words: 'they are too busy saving the souls of white Christians from future burning in hell-fire to save the lives of black ones from present burning in flames kindled by the white Christians.'

By the time tea was finished Mary had learned much that she never knew about the plight of black Americans. She promised to hold a drawing room meeting for Ida at her London house the following week, but in the event she did more than that. She funded a meeting at the Ideal Club for Ida's final address, which was delivered to a 'large and influential concourse', including some members of Parliament. One of these insisted on organising a breakfast for Ida the following day at the Westminster Palace Hotel. Sixteen more MPs turned up, bringing their wives. As Ida talked to them, at 'beautifully decorated tables', she passed around a picture of the lynching of CJ Miller in Kentucky, a man murdered for a crime which he did not commit. (I hope it put them off their breakfast.) Before Ida left England a London Anti-Lynching Committee had been formed.

Lynching of C. J. Miller, at Bardwell, Kentucky, July 7th, 1893.

I'd like to be able to say that my ancestors were abolitionists, but sadly can find nothing to support this. However, in their inimitably inconsistent way they held certain principles where the underprivileged were concerned. I discovered that almost a hundred years earlier Mary's great-grandfather had made himself extremely unpopular with plantation owners on Barbados, by insisting on the humane treatment of slaves.

Francis Humberston Mackenzie, last Earl of Seaforth, had done what many a financially pinched aristocrat did in those days – he took up the post of governor to a Caribbean colony for five or so years, which happened to be the years immediately before the Abolition of Slave Trade Act of 1807. The white planters who had been there for several generations were outraged when the newly arrived governor, who understood nothing about their lives, forced through legislation that made the penalty for killing a black slave the same as that for killing a white person: death. This was a big step-up from a fine of £11 4s – which anyway was rarely imposed. Worse, he insisted on the provision of medical treatment for slaves, and even wrote letters home detailing atrocities he'd witnessed being visited upon them.

Not that Seaforth ever contested the right of the white man to own a slave. His governor's salary turned out to be disappointingly modest – for a start, the simple expense of importing a decent wine cellar to Barbados consumed nearly a sixth of it, and a man in his position clearly had standards to maintain. So to boost his income he invested in a couple of slave plantations at Berbice in British Guiana (now Guyana). Although he never went there, managing his properties remotely, he sentimentally named them Brahan and Kintail, after his Scottish estates.

Henry Hyndman, whose grandfather also owned a plantation at Berbice, claims that slaves here had a reasonable standard of living. They could get a good education, and their working hours were limited by law to 45 hours a week. Indeed he went on to compare their lives favourably with those of white children working at the other end of the trade, in cotton mills in Cheshire, and maybe he had a point. However it is unlikely that life for the black workers was quite as utopian as Hyndman suggests, since it did not stop one of Seaforth's slaves (a man called Inverness!) from trying to escape.

So let us skate over this uncomfortable morsel of history and return to Mary and Ida chatting over afternoon tea. I can't help feeling that they would have found much in common. As well as a background in journalism, they shared a firmness of opinion which in Ida's case was viewed as brazen outspokenness, earning her the disapproval even of her fellow civil rights activists. Mary, of course, could get away with it. They both liked to dress in a very respectable fashion – for Ida this was essential, as where she came from black women could be treated as whores. And, coincidentally, although Ida was seventeen years younger than Mary, both women were to die in the same year, 1931, both by then largely forgotten.

I would never have known about any of this had Ida not been lifted from obscurity in 2020 by being honoured with a posthumous Pulitzer Prize special citation for her 'outstanding and courageous reporting on the horrific and vicious violence against African Americans during the era of lynching'. It was at this point that someone added the bare fact that Ida had 'had tea with Lady Jeune' to Mary's Wikipedia page, giving me yet another avenue to explore.

Ida sent accounts of her British tour back to the *Daily Inter Ocean* newspaper of Chicago. These were mostly very favourable, as she was warmly welcomed wherever she went. She was interviewed by Keir Hardie, who showed her both houses of Parliament, and was taken to visit feminist novelist Sarah Grand. She had two complaints – the weather in June was near freezing, and she did not like English railway carriages: '...

knees rubbing against those of entire strangers, and being forced to stare into each other's faces for hours, are almost intolerable and would be quite so, were the English not uniformly so courteous as they are,' she wrote. At the same time she very much appreciated being able to travel in trains 'free from insult or discrimination on account of color'. But a definite highlight of her tour, picked out as a heading, was her 'Very Pleasant Afternoon with Lady Jeune.'

An Unreliable Witness

*In which Mary provides fruitful connections for Frank Harris
and abundant material for his memoirs*

Frank Harris, diminutive pioneer of tabloid journalism, was not universally loved or admired, however much his memoirs might try to persuade you otherwise. He was generally seen as an objectionable little man whose career was built on gossip, one who, George Bernard Shaw remarked, 'blazed through London like a comet, leaving a trail of deeply annoyed persons behind him'. This may be the only reason he was not included in Mary's 1909 *Memories of Fifty Years*, for the salacious autobiography for which he is mainly remembered today was not published until 1922. He seems to have been a frequent visitor to Mary's house, at one stage (he claims) being invited there once a week. This was quite possibly true during the period when he was editing the *Fortnightly* or *Saturday Reviews*, and commissioning articles from her.

It was Mary who instigated Harris' friendship with Oscar Wilde. He had often seen Oscar at what he called 'Mrs Jeune's *omnium gatherums*', but had been avoiding him for ages, repelled by 'something oily and fat about him', and by Oscar's determination 'to astonish and dazzle.' But one evening, as Harris arrived at her front door, Mary collared him, saying, 'Have you ever met Mr Oscar Wilde? You ought to know him: he is so delightfully clever, so brilliant!' At this Harris could hardly refuse to shake Oscar's 'flabby' hand, or to follow him into an inner room where they could talk without being disturbed.

In half an hour Harris had revised his opinion of Oscar. He was 'surprised' he said, 'first of all by the kindness of his literary and artistic judgments and then by his wit and humour'. A friendship was born that would endure through Oscar's fall from grace nearly ten years later, for Harris, whatever his defects, stood by his friend when others had abandoned him.

Less successful were Mary's attempts to improve relations between Harris and Lady Colin Campbell, who had been a victim of his tabloid sensationalism. In 1886 Lady Colin found herself barred from fashionable drawing rooms (with the exception, of course, of Mary Jeune's) following a divorce trial in which she was the innocent party, but which attracted extremely lurid reportage – none more so than in the *Evening News*, of which Frank Harris was editor at the time.

Lady Colin was born Gertrude Blood, a dark-eyed beauty who got engaged after a short romance with the very well-connected Lord Colin Campbell. Her mother was delighted by the match, which would bring Gertrude a notch or two up the social scale, but her father had misgivings when Lord Colin kept postponing the marriage. He had a suspicion that Colin was suffering from 'that loathsome disease' – and, far too late, it turned out that he was right. After the marriage finally took place poor Gertrude was infected with syphilis. She applied for a judicial separation, as a woman could not instigate divorce.

The unrepentant Colin retaliated by suing for divorce on grounds of her alleged adultery, and the details of the case were splashed all over the newspapers and devoured by the general public. One of Colin's witnesses claimed to have viewed Lady Colin's adultery through a keyhole, giving rise to the immortal phrase 'What the butler saw'. Still, there were certain things that you could not mention in the newspapers, one of them being venereal disease. Only Harris was bold enough to print witness statements verbatim, including the dreaded word 'syphilis', upon which the *Evening News* was immediately sued for obscene libel by the National Vigilance Association. In spite of the fact that Harris' colourful reporting of the trial had doubled the paper's circulation, he was sent packing.

Gertrude was in a difficult position. No adultery was proved, so no divorce granted, and now she was shunned by polite society. Mary, however, took her under her wing. She thought that the least Harris could do after helping to make her a pariah was to offer her some work, for Gertrude was a sharp observer and gifted with the pen.

Mary arranged for Harris to meet her at Harley Street, but the assignment did not get off to a good start. When Mary showed him into the drawing room, Gertrude was holding up her skirt and 'toasting her legs in front of the fire'. It was just not done for women to show their ankles, and Harris later claimed that this was a come-on. I think it's more likely that he made an advance which was rejected. He did apologise to her for his paper having offended her at the time of the divorce case, and invited her to write for him on any subject she liked – but he never published more than one article. Behind her back he referred to her as 'that fat-arsed bitch'.

It was almost certainly his loss. In the opinion of Bernard Shaw she was 'a lady with a lightning wit, a merciless sense of humour, a skill in journalism surpassing that of any interviewer…' Anyway, Gertrude managed to succeed without Harris' help, and pursued a profitable career writing articles under various pseudonyms to disguise her identity. A book called *A Woman's Walks* combined her travels around Europe with explorations through grubby back gardens in south London, while her articles proposed such progressive notions as bicycle lanes on main roads, and equal rights for women smokers. The 'loathsome disease' cut her life short, and she died in 1911 aged only 54. It took ten years after that for her portrait to be displayed in the National Portrait Gallery, as she was still considered a disgrace.

Getting fired from the *Evening News* doesn't seem to have done Harris the slightest harm, as he then went on to edit the *Fortnightly Review*, a classier publication altogether. It boasted a high calibre of contributors, including Mary of course. However, an article which appeared to promote assassination as an acceptable form of political activism caused more of a stir than the proprietors felt quite comfortable with, and in 1894 he was asked to move on.

He became editor at the *Saturday Review* where his first action was to sack all the staff and take on such literary luminaries as George Bernard Shaw, Max Beerbohm and H.G. Wells, turning it into one of the best periodicals in town. He was still commissioning articles from Mary, whose subject matter by this time had segued from social issues to Society issues. The '*Saturday Reviler*', as it was known by some, was as sharp-tongued and hard-hitting as its editor, and did not improve his popularity.

Possibly to compensate for his small size (5ft 5in without his cuban heels), Harris had an aggressive demeanour and a voice like a chainsaw that could cut through the loudest conversations. At lunch at the Savile Club he brayed: 'I suppose that one cannot expect in this assembly of faded prigs to find a glass of good wine.' That cost him an invitation to join the Tory party, though as he had spent years waging a vendetta against the ruling classes he probably didn't care.

At Mary's however, her peculiar knack of maintaining equanimity all round meant that he could get away with remarks of this sort. William H. Rideing, editor of the *North American Review*, was astonished to witness Harris exercising his freedom of expression at one of her dinners where there were a number of peers present.

> An aggressive and satirical young man who edited one of the leading English reviews declared: "There's nothing I enjoy more than rejecting an article by a member of the House of Lords. He's sure to be a duffer!' Did their lordships bridle and darken? Did the others show anxiety – the hostess alarm? Not a bit of it. Everybody laughed.

It was Merlin Holland, Oscar Wilde's grandson, who recommended that I take the plunge into Harris' *My Life and Loves*.

I had emailed him to ask if he knew of any more correspondence between his grandfather and my great-great-grandmother. He said he didn't – but that there were a few mentions of her in Harris' raunchy autobiography, which was banned in England and America for forty years, and inspired a volume of rebuttals called *Lies and Libels of Frank Harris*. I was surprised to think that Mary might feature in this semi-pornographic oeuvre. 'Don't you mean *Oscar Wilde: his Life and Confessions?*' I asked. No, he replied, he meant *My Life and Loves*, and so I soon found myself slinking shamefacedly out of the central library in Bristol with the enormous tome hidden under my coat.

The last time I'd seen this book was in my school days, when it was passed around secretly by my friends as the only sex education on offer. You had to skip many tedious pages about politicians you'd never heard of to get to the next dirty bit. Now I was doing the opposite: I had to skip many a steamy encounter to find glimpses of my great-great-grandmother. Luckily Holland had recommended a particular edition that had an index, which saved me from many hours of unwelcome stimulation.

Harris plainly spent many hours round at Mary's, for he reported a variety of unusual goings-on which appear in other chapters of this book, particularly those involving Randolph Churchill. They make for entertaining reading, for Harris was never one to sacrifice a good yarn for the sake of accuracy – 'I'm an artist, not a reporter', he said. He paints an engaging picture of an evening at Mary's house – there, he says, you could witness:

> Prince Edward talking to Hyndman, the socialist agitator, while Lord Wolseley and Herbert Bismarck listened eagerly intent; at the same time near the fireplace Arthur Balfour, Henry Irving and Theodore Roosevelt hung on the lips of Whistler, who was telling a story.

Harris was present at a lunch party at Mary's soon after Oscar

Wilde's trial. The newspapers had had a field day with his demise, with the exception of *Reynolds News* which refused 'to gloat over the ruin of the unhappy man.' In the society where Oscar had once been lionised, Harris noted that 'the mere mention of his name was met with expressions of disgust, or frozen silence.'

Whatever his personal shortcomings, he has to be credited with being one of the few people who stuck by Oscar and was not afraid to defend him in public. At Mary's luncheon the disgraced playwright was the topic of conversation, and some of her guests were crowing over Oscar's conviction. One was glad that Oscar was getting what he deserved, another thought that two years' hard labour was too lenient. A third, unnamed guest

> intimated delicately and with quiet complacence that two year's imprisonment with hard labour usually resulted in idiocy or death... 'You were an intimate friend of his, were you not?' insinuated the delicate one gently. 'A friend and admirer,' I replied, 'and always shall be.'
>
> A glacial silence spread round the table, while the delicate one smiled with deprecating contempt, and offered some grapes to his neighbour; but help came. Lady Dorothy Nevill was a little further down the table: she had not heard all that was said, but had caught the tone of the conversation and divined the rest.
>
> 'Are you talking of Oscar Wilde?' she exclaimed. 'I'm glad to hear you say you are a friend. I am, too, and shall always be proud of having known him, a most brilliant, charming man.'
>
> 'I think of giving a dinner to him when he comes out, Lady Dorothy,' I said.
>
> 'I hope you'll ask me,' she answered bravely. 'I should be glad to come. I always admired and liked him; I feel dreadfully sorry for him.'

Of course Lady Dorothy was no stranger to scandal herself, having in her youth been caught in a summerhouse with an aristocratic rake who refused to make an honest woman of her. She was forced to claw back some respectability by marrying an elderly cousin who provided her with six children – though at least one of them was rumoured to have been fathered by Disraeli.

Mary was perhaps too far down the table to contribute to the discussion, but sitting next to Harris was her daughter Madeleine, who would have been not quite nineteen. She turned to him and said 'I wish I had known him, there must have been great good in him to win such friendship.' It seems a little unlikely that Madeleine had not known such a frequent visitor to the house. But then, as Max Beerbohm commented, Harris stuck to the facts 'only when his invention flagged'.

The New Woman and the Bicycle

In which Mary doubts that New Woman is the 'most brilliant development of this most original age', although the bicycle definitely is

By the last decade of the 19th century it was clear that women's lives were getting better. Wives now had some basic rights, while an increasing number of women were attending university, even if they were not necessarily given a degree at the end of it. They sensed some promise of freedom ahead, like a faint light dawning over a rather misty horizon. What form it would take no-one quite knew – perhaps women would even get to vote one day. Some reacted with hope, others with fear, and out of this uncertainty was born a novel phenomenon: the New Woman, a creature almost impossible to pigeonhole.

Anyone who wants to study the debates surrounding her will not be short of material – today there are countless academic theses on the subject as well as enough books to furnish a feminist's study. For instance, there are no less than FIVE volumes of *The Late-Victorian Marriage Question: A Collection of Key New Woman Texts* (Routledge 1998).

It would be futile to try and cover the topic in one chapter of this book, but needless to say Mary Jeune was to be found at the epicentre of the debate, and indeed has to be credited with inventing the term New Woman (a fact that has escaped most experts on the subject). It was in 1889 that an article by Lady Catherine Gaskell about the trials of modern womanhood got Mary going. Lady Catherine was complaining about how terribly busy life had become for today's woman, now that better education meant that she was expected to be not only domestically proficient, but also well-informed. Mary's response to it was damning.

What provoked her was that Lady Catherine was only talking about women of her own class (the upper). Mary's rejoinder, in an essay entitled 'Women of To-day, Yesterday, and To-morrow' in the *National Review*, began by pouring scorn on the idea that such women were in any way typical – they were the 'few abnormal products of modern society. They can be counted almost on one's fingers', she declared. She then proceeded to point out that it was actually the servants who did all the work in these women's houses, and that their lives were incomparably much easier than that of women thirty years earlier. Education, she said, had done nothing but good for countless middle-class women who could now engage in the professions.

Returning to a favourite theme, she turned on her own peer group: '…it is becoming the fashion for women of the upper classes to lead lives of excitement and unrest, it cannot fail to spread, and the injury it will inflict on the nation is certain to be serious.' Finally she dismissed the whole idea that the female was evolving as a passing fad: 'the new woman, with her political aspirations, her religious opinions, and her advanced social theories, will play a prominent though perhaps not lovely part… the hot fit of excitement will pass, and reason will reassert its sway.'

When this essay was republished five years later her New Woman had cannily acquired capital letters. For by then the debate had been revived and injected with fresh vigour by writers Sarah Grand and Ouida, in a pair of articles in the *North American Review*. The two women took up opposing stances. Grand was a progressive feminist who had spent years campaigning against the Contagious Diseases Act and promoting female suffrage. Ouida, by contrast, was the author of a raft of successful swashbuckling romances, with little empathy or even tolerance for the tribulations of her sisters.

Grand was born Frances Clarke, but renamed herself when she

wrote her humorous and highly transgressive novel, *The Heavenly Twins*. It breached many Victorian taboos with its audacious cross-gender experiments, irreverent pokes at religion, and a husband who gives his wife and baby syphilis. It was far too controversial for any publisher to take on, so Grand raised the money from friends and acquaintances and published it herself. It was an instant best-seller and threw up a storm. Reviewers said it was nasty-minded and coarse, and Grand was shunned by Society, but she had her supporters – Angela Burdett Coutts sent round a footman with a note: 'Fear not, you have powerful friends'.

Mary thought it a book one would not want one's daughters to read; nevertheless she had to admit that it was more entertaining than *Northanger Abbey*. She felt obliged to level some criticism at its author: 'That woman doesn't know what she wants. She doesn't know what she is talking about. She is in favour of free love!' When Grand heard of this she seemed to be more amused than upset. 'It was as if she [Mary] had said that I advocated curried babies for luncheon,' she remarked. 'But she's a very amiable person generally...' And indeed they seem to have got on quite well, Mary later praising Grand as the 'most brilliant and versatile of advocates' for the New Woman, towards whom by this time her feelings were beginning to soften.

In 1898, nearly ten years after her first broadside, she was admitting that 'it has been our fortune to come into contact with many New Women' – in fact, she said, 'we cannot see where the difference exists between the New and the Old, except it be in the matter of her trousers'.

Ouida on the other hand was strongly opposed to anything that threatened traditional ideas of femininity, especially mixed schooling, women in politics, and women taking long train journeys alone – unless they were rich enough to pay for a first-class compartment, and could avoid the disgrace of 'sleeping in odious vicinity to strangers on a shelf.' She liked to dress in the flouncy costumes her fictional heroines might have worn, which didn't suit her at all as she was very short with a rather masculine demeanour.

Mary enjoyed Ouida's novels, though, like Sarah Grand's, she judged them as being 'just beyond the high water-mark of books that could be safely admitted to the family library'. She was thrilled when a friend took her to meet the novelist. This friend, unnamed in Mary's memoir, was almost certainly Oscar Wilde. He was a great fan of Ouida, and unashamedly copied her epigrammatic style.

Mary went to visit Ouida at the Langham Hotel, where the novelist had become legendary for spending her winters lying in bed with the curtains drawn in a room illuminated by candles, writing purple prose on violet-coloured notepaper, and surrounded by masses of purple flowers. Mary expected to see 'a graceful woman of middle age, with traces of great beauty.' But she was in for a shock. When she arrived in Ouida's crepuscular room, she says, 'surprise and disappointment can hardly convey my feelings… Small, insignificant-looking, with no pretension to beauty, her harsh voice, and manner almost grotesque in its affectation, completed the destruction of my ideal.'

In spite of this setback Mary and Ouida kept in touch, corresponding on subjects in which they shared an interest – especially the Woman Question. Unfortunately Ouida's letters ended up like most of Mary's correspondence. They were 'so dangerously amusing', she says, 'that their only possible fate was to be consigned to the flames.' Having said this, two letters did survive in the family archive, providing material evidence that Ouida did indeed favour purple ink. Her copperplate handwriting is so extravagantly large that she can barely fit three words to a line – her manuscripts must have been a publisher's nightmare.

The New Woman inhabited two very different personae. In the press, she was derided as a smoking, trouser-wearing harridan, to be avoided at all costs. But in the literature of the period she was treated with sympathy, and a raft of new novels, loosely classed by their detractors as 'anti-marriage', were attracting a wide readership. They were not afraid to take on the issues of the day: Mona Caird's *The Wings of Azrael* (marital rape and husband murder); Ella Hepworth Dixon's *Story of a Modern Woman* (who *chooses* to stay single); *A Yellow Aster* by 'Iota', Irish writer Kathleen Caffyn (woman who chooses a love-child over a loveless marriage). Even men were getting in on the act: Grant Allen, George Gissing, and of course Thomas Hardy. It's hardly surprising that Mary as a journalist, but at the same time friend of many of these novelists, found herself conflicted.

Sarah Grand's view was nuanced, rather than conflicted. She concluded her 1894 essay 'The New Aspect of the Woman Question' with this statement: 'The Woman Question is the Marriage Question, as shall be shown hereafter.' Indeed, she had hit the nail on the head. A few years earlier an article in the *Westminster Review*, innocuously entitled 'Marriage', had set a bomb under that sacred institution. Its author, Mona Caird, dared to decry marriage for life as 'a vexatious failure', and to compare the fate of a wife to that of a chained dog. She called for relaxation of the divorce laws and appeared to condone free love.

Caird herself had managed to avoid many of the drawbacks of marriage by getting hitched to a gentleman farmer in Scotland who allowed her plenty of free rein. She spent more time in London than at home in Kirkcudbright, often at Mary Jeune's table. Others were not so fortunate.

In the summer of 1888 the *Telegraph* reacted to Caird's article by asking its readers 'Is Marriage a Failure?' This opened the floodgates to years of suppressed rancour which came bubbling up through its columns. The question elicited more than 27,000 handwritten replies. According to Harry Quilter, who published a selection of them later in the year, 'the Editor's table disappeared beneath the varieties of experience, and England stood aghast at the mass of correspondence, which, like a snow-ball, grew in size as it rolled along.' Opinions poured in from all over Europe, America, the colonies, even Japan. Based mainly on the correspondents' personal experiences, they ranged from 'any woman is a fool, and any man a criminal, who tries to tamper with an institution which has always been held sacred' to 'I entreat you, sisters, to be slaves no longer.'

Many of the respondents had not actually read Caird's original article, which ended on an optimistic note: 'we look forward steadily, hoping and working for the day when men and women shall be comrades and fellow-workers as well as lovers and husbands and wives...' Mary had already managed to achieve this pleasant arrangement, therefore it is no surprise that she was a strong supporter of matrimony and wasted no time in writing to the *Telegraph* to tell them so. As far as she was concerned, marriage was 'the beginning of a relation of which mutual affection, fidelity and forbearance are the bases,' and that since it was part of the fabric of society 'any attempt to meddle or interfere with it will bring the whole thing about our ears.'

But the seeds of doubt had been sown. By 1894 the press was bristling with new magazines aimed at women, whether married or single, who had opinions. Ranging from the candidly feminist *Woman's Penny Paper* to the mildly progressive *Young Woman*, they provided a forum for a wide range of viewpoints, and the woman/marriage discussion was providing plenty of copy. *Young Woman* decided to commission a series from celebrity writers on 'An Ideal Husband', at the same time that Wilde was writing his play of the same name. Of course Wilde's play used the term ironically – even more ironically, he dedicated it to Frank Harris, a less ideal husband than whom one can hardly imagine.

As an established authority on the issue, Mary was invited to contribute. Her piece in *Young Woman* started out boldly enough: 'Woman in her new found strength is redressing the inequalities of four thousand years and demanding a recognition at the hands of her former lord and master of the position of equality she has taken up...' But after that she seemed lost for words to describe any way in which a husband might be ideal, and instead turned her attention to the wives whose task it was to 'make the men they lived with better…not by preaching, abuse or vituperation, but by making their own example…and by the subtle influence they possess'.

Twenty years later Mary had hardly shifted her position on the wife's role. Addressing the London Girls' Club Union in 1914 she offered a pragmatic approach: 'It may be true that husbands are poor creatures, but the wives' lives are happier when they attend to the creature comforts of the breadwinner of the family.'

Meanwhile her friend Thomas Hardy was writing a book that would seriously put a cat among the pigeons. Mary knew about this because it had been incubating for the past eight years, and she had spent many a cosy evening with him around the fire listening to the ideas for his novels. Mona Caird was often there too, expounding her radical views on marriage. Hardy records how they 'talked of the marriage laws… also the difficulties of separation, of terminable marriages where there are children, and the nervous strain of living with a man when you know he can throw you over at any moment.'

At Arlington Manor Hardy would go for walks through the woods with Francis Jeune, and the two men would exchange their thoughts on the subject of divorce. He could hardly have found a higher authority to consult on the finer points of the law, as Francis was now Chief Justice of the divorce courts. In this role he was frequently required to preside over cases of 'collusion'. Because adultery was the only allowable grounds for divorce, couples who wished to part amicably would often collude in giving false evidence of an adultery that had never actually happened. Francis would chuckle over these stories, which he related to Hardy as they strolled, but as an official upholder of the law he was obliged to dismiss such cases. He had no power to change the law, he could only recommend temporary separation to mitigate the pain of marital conflict. Meanwhile Hardy's strong belief was that 'a marriage should be dissolvable as soon as it becomes a cruelty to either of the parties'.

Mary was not only aware of Hardy's plans for his 'new woman' novel, she was to some extent embroiled in them. A year before *Jude the Obscure* was published he had asked her to come to the defence of *Life's little Ironies*, a collection of short stories which was strongly criticised for introducing 'a note of sensuality' into English fiction. At his request Mary wrote to the *Daily Chronicle* to vouch that she could not recall 'one story that can offend the most sensitive morality,' signing herself 'A Mother' (though when it was published they couldn't resist printing her name).

Her support was clearly important to Hardy, and he must have known that Mary would have a problem with Sue Brideshead's determination to shun the sacrament of marriage for no very obvious reason. Indeed I'm afraid that Mary's strongly-held views on the subject may be responsible for Sue Brideshead's humiliating descent into the twin shackles of marriage and religion, and possibly even for the death of all those children…

Whatever influence she may have had in cutting Sue down to size, it was all in vain. On publication, *Jude the Obscure* was immediately classed as an 'anti-marriage' novel and fiercely attacked in the press. *Harper's* American edition agreed to serialise it, but only if Sue's bastard children were changed into adopted orphans!

Amazingly, Hardy doesn't seem to have predicted any of this. He wrote an ingenuous letter to his friend George Douglas: 'you can imagine my surprise at the Guardian saying that everything sacred is brought into contempt, &c. in the novel! Did you see that The World nearly fainted away, & the Pall Mall went into fits over the story?' Hardy's old friend Edmund Gosse upset him by saying to his face that *Jude* was 'the most indecent novel ever written'. In his review Gosse wrote: 'What has Providence done to Mr Hardy that he should rise up in the arable land of Wessex and shake his fist at his Creator?'

The Bishop of Wakefield burned a copy of the book and announced his action to the world, prompting a number of other readers to do the same and send Hardy the ashes. It was beginning to look like the Victorian equivalent of *The Satanic Verses*.

At lunch at Mary's one day, Hardy briefly lost his normally quiet demeanour. He took up a native American war club and, wielding it with some difficulty, said: 'How much I should like to have that in my hand when I encounter the critic who calls *Jude the Obscure* Jude the Obscene!' (What he failed to realise, though everyone else did, was that he had just been sitting next to that very critic – a woman.) He wrote Mary a long letter of injured innocence:

> You will have seen how "Jude" has been attacked in two or three quarters. I am much surprised at the nature of the attack… As to the "marriage question" I wonder they do not see that my own opinions are nowhere given: indeed I felt that by the heroine's recantation of all her views, at the end of the story, & becoming a penance-seeking Christian, I was almost too High-Churchy.

It is no surprise that at this point Hardy decided to give up novel-writing for good, and retreat to writing poetry for the rest of his life.

The same year that *Jude* was published saw Oscar Wilde's fall from grace. This resulted in the New Woman, by association, being dropped by the press like a hot potato. Dandified men and women in Rational Dress suddenly lost their appeal. But the marriage debate did not go away, and continued to rumble on through the nineties. Mary was asked to write a piece on 'The Modern Marriage Market', and four essays on this subject were gathered into a slim volume by Marie Corelli, best-selling author of mystical and melodramatic works of fiction.

Born Marie Mackay, Corelli was the model for E.F. Benson's Lucia, a vain and snobbish woman who pretends she can speak Italian. When Oscar Wilde was asked by a friendly jailer in Reading Gaol what he thought of the popular novelist's work, he answered, 'Now don't think that I have anything against her moral character, but from the way she writes she ought to be here.'

The first essay in the *The Modern Marriage Market* is Corelli's, and its message is that romantic love should be the *only* basis for marriage. She could well afford to promote this view as she herself was not married and lived happily with a woman for 46 years. What she lacked in intellectual rigour she made up for with a baroque literary style: 'What of the Season', she asked, 'when women are as coolly "brought out" to be sold as any unhappy Armenian girl that ever shuddered at the lewd gaze of a Turkish tyrant?'

Another essay in the collection is by Flora Annie Steel, a writer who had spent 22 years in the Punjab campaigning for educational and other reforms. She observed that although marriages there were arranged, 'the percentage of rational happiness derived from wifehood and motherhood is as high in India as it is in England'. For her love was not part of the equation: 'Why I married I cannot say: I have never been able to say. I do not think either of us was in love. I know I was not: I never have been.'

Mary's contribution fell, both physically and ideologically, between these two, and was characteristically pragmatic: 'Love in a cottage is a delicious thing, but the wherewithal to provide the cottage and its accessories is an absolute necessity.' Luckily her new son-in-law Henry Allhusen, heir to an industrialist's fortune, was able to provide a home that was substantially more than a cottage for Dorothy, and their happy union was clearly influencing Mary's views. When the *Idler* magazine ran a series on 'Early Marriages – should they be encouraged or abolished?' Mary came out strongly in favour, insisting that 'the marriage which always seems to hold out the best promise of happiness is that where a man is thirty and a woman some ten years younger' – the exact ages of Henry and Dorothy.

Having had the last word on marriage, Mary turned her attention to the craze that was sweeping the country – the bicycle. The arrival of this machine on the mass market was now improving life for thousands of women. It was affordable for all but the very poorest,

Bicycle face

offered unprecedented freedom and independence, and was fast becoming a symbol of female emancipation.

Of course this prompted a variety of 'medical experts' (i.e. men) to warn against the dangers of ladies exerting themselves, and possibly damaging the 'feminine organs of matrimonial necessity'. There was the added danger of 'bicycle face', described by a certain Dr Shadwell as 'an aerodynamic head with a pinched face, pointed nose, slack jaw, beady eyes, features pulled back, and permanently frazzled expression.'

Eliza Lynn Lynton, vociferous opponent of the New Woman, warned against the 'intoxication which comes with unfettered liberty.' But it was too late: the bicycle was here to stay. And Mary was one of the first women in London to ride a bike, listing her hobbies in 'Who's Who' as cycling, skating, and riding, in that order.

Her interest in the bicycle had begun when Oliver Stanton, a young American with an engineering background, came to stay at

Arlington Manor for the weekend. He had started riding a bicycle at home in the States, but was told on arriving in England that 'the nicest people did not cycle.' Mary however was fascinated by the idea and asked Stanton to teach Francis how to ride. This was such a success that she urged Stanton to take up teaching as a profession.

In a very short space of time public disapproval shifted away from people who cycled to people who did not, and Stanton was giving private lessons in the Botanical Gardens in Regent's Park, advertising such specialist skills as 'mounting and dismounting taught by an entirely new method.' In due course he went on to teach the Prince of Wales, starting him off on the back of a tandem in Cannes.

Cycling was taken up by Society and other celebrities, and a common sight in the early mornings was that of a crowd of bicycles on Battersea Bridge, heading for the Park. On one famous occasion George Bernard Shaw, who never quite mastered the art of cycling, crashed into Bertrand Russell. He harboured some notion that vegetarianism rendered one impregnable, and indeed it was Russell's machine (and knickerbockers) that sustained most of the damage, while Shaw, who had flown twenty feet through the air, walked away unhurt. Russell had to catch the train home, and the relationship between the two men was not improved by Shaw out-cycling the train and poking his head into Russell's carriage at each station stop, in order to jeer at him. But generally the bicycle was a force for good. Even the Hardys got on a bit better after they acquired bicycles and pedalled the Dorset byways together.

Mary wrote an article extolling the joys of cycling for the *Badminton Magazine of Sports and Pastimes*. In her opinion it was a sport that was beneficial to the health and well-being of all women, provided one could find suitable clothing – which prompted another article, this time on 'What is the Best Cycling Dress for Women?' in *The Woman at Home*.

The subject of what to wear on a bicycle provoked almost as much controversy as the New Woman had. The bloomer or 'freedom dress' had enjoyed a brief craze back in the fifties, but it had been roundly ridiculed and had faded from view. Now on offer were knickerbockers, generally discounted for being far too manly, or the 'knicker skirt', a voluminous divided dress elasticated below the knee, and recommended by The Rational Dress Society. However women had to be very brave to go out in these ungainly bags. Their wearers were denounced from the pulpit, and when riding through the rougher parts of town they risked being verbally abused or even manhandled off their steeds. As late as 1898 Lady Harberton, founder of the Rational Dress Society, was refused service at a hotel when she turned up in her baggy knickers.

For these reasons Rational Dress did not really catch on – following Lady Jeune's guidelines was much safer. The female body was clearly not designed to wear a trouser, she said, and therefore she recommended 'a grey skirt of double Melton' – which would not

Here is a photograph from the family album, of Mary wearing the correct outfit for cycling. I worry that the skirt reaching to within three inches of the ground may get caught in the chain. Mary's composure is so complete that I suspect the photo has been posed – though how they got the bicycle to remain upright while stationary is a mystery...

show the dirt – three inches from the ground. Flannel, she said, was essential. 'A thin flannel shirt, stays lined with thin flannel, and a thin flannel blouse over it all, is the ideal dress for bicycling.' Like Lady Bracknell, on this point, as on all points, she was sure.

Mary Jeune's Dosser

*In which Mary provides a bolt-hole for Thomas Hardy
and an escape from Emma, while he becomes
Uncle Tom to her daughters*

Mary's memoir devotes barely a page to Thomas Hardy, and says very little that everyone doesn't know already. (By contrast, his letters are full of references to her, and perhaps the most fruitful source of detail about her life.) She starts like this: 'For many years of his literary career Mr Hardy was very little in London, and society had no attractions for him.' This may be true, but for the last decade of the century he was very often in London, and his favourite place to stay was with Mary and Francis. He could often be observed, towards the end of one of Mary's parties, creeping up the stairs to his room. He was christened 'the dosser' by Lord Rowton, a man who knew all about dossers, having set up a series of lodging houses for workers in London where you could get clean sheets and hot water for just sixpence a night.

Hardy, of course, didn't pay anything for the same privilege at Mary Jeune's, where he was also assured of a warm welcome. It's not hard to see that it was more appealing than gloomy Max Gate with a sullen Emma in the attic. Here he found himself in the bosom of a happy family, and not having any children of his own, he delighted in the company of Madeleine and Dorothy, who when he first met them were not yet ten years old. He loved taking them to the theatre, and they loved him back, calling him Uncle Tom. He remained a faithful friend to Dorothy until the day he died.

Although Hardy had a reputation for shyness, he plainly liked rubbing shoulders with Mary's more distinguished guests. He can't resist boasting to Emma when he meets the Chancellor of the

Exchequer at breakfast, or when his companion 'lodger' is Queen Victoria's grandson, Prince Albert Victor. Then there were the weekend house parties at Arlington Manor, with more high-profile guests, and evening entertainments in the form of comedy sketches from George Grossmith, or am-drams in which the whole Jeune family acted. 'There was never another house like it for cheerfulness', he said.

Hardy first mentions Mary in 1885, summing her up with a single adjective: 'irrepressible'. That was the year she had her first articles published, 'Helping the Fallen' and 'Saving the Innocents'. Was it a shared interest in fallen women that brought them together? Mary had been interviewing unmarried mothers for a rescue home in Kilburn for the last ten years, and these first essays were based on her experience. They were properly researched and backed up with statistics, for it was important, she said, to divest oneself 'of any wish to look at the sentimental or morbid side of the matter'. She then proceeded to completely ignore her own advice in this description of everyday life in the workhouse:

> 'Fifty or sixty children, from a month to three years old, the majority of whom were wan, ill, unhealthy, with the careworn expression of old people, or the wistful look of suffering, were a spectacle not easily effaced from memory… and, saddest, perhaps, of all, the long row of little low chairs, into which were strapped five or six children, old enough to sit up, but not strong enough to walk who, with eager eyes, looked for someone to lift them out…'

This chimed a powerful note with Hardy, who sent Mary a copy of his *Mayor of Casterbridge* with a note saying:

> The intention of the story will not be missed by the writer of those pathetic and striking articles which appeared from your pen in the Fortnightly last year. The picture you drew of the 'row of little chairs' lingers in my mind still.

By 1890 they were firm friends and he had become used to staying at Wimpole Street. Hardy's fallen woman, Tess of the D'Urbervilles, was just about to hit the shelves and prompt many women who had suffered like her to write to him for advice. (Francis Jeune advised him NOT to respond.) Mary meanwhile was confiding in him that she was less sure of her opinions than the tone of her journalism might suggest.

> Mary Jeune says that when she tries to convey some sort of moral or religious teaching to the East-end poor, so as to change their views from wrong to right, it ends by their convincing her that their view is the right one – not by her convincing them.

He was impressed by her stamina, observing how she rushed off to the East End the morning after a big party, even though a second party was due the same evening – 'She says that when you are strong like her, it is really not so much to do as it seems.' (He also notes her parsimony: 'She says she wasted a shilling this morning by taking a cab, usually going in penny omnibuses.')

Shy and retiring he may have been, but Hardy didn't seem to object to being dragged by the Jeunes to entertainments of a nature far more frivolous than his own. One night Mary had some guests who 'stayed as if they would never go.' When the last one did finally leave, they

> rushed off to Lord Stanhope's in Grosvenor Place, arrived about half past twelve, had a charming hob-and-nob time, everybody but four being gone, and reaching bed about two o'clock.

Another night Mary and Francis took Hardy 'suddenly off after dinner' to the Music Hall where Lottie Collins was performing *Ta-ra-ra Boom-de-ay*, which she had made her signature song. She would start off very quietly and gradually crescendo into a rousing chorus, accompanied with a can-can dance that drove the audience wild. The normally reserved Hardy was surprised to find himself singing, or rather shouting, along at the top of his voice.

These adventures he did not confess to his wife, but to Florence Henniker who was now becoming his correspondent of choice. His letters to Emma, by contrast, are painful in their attempts to make his London life sound less appealing. 'This morning at breakfast Mrs and Mr Jeune both pressed me to stay over to-morrow' he writes, casually adding, 'Irving and Ellen Terry are coming to dine with them to-morrow: and I felt I might as well stay on'.

Another time, with feigned indifference, he writes 'I *think* that before I come back I will go and stay at the Jeunes' for a day or two – if they can have me.' Meanwhile Mary was unfailingly polite in extending her invitations to Emma. Hardy passed these on: 'She is very kind and nice, and says that if you have to come to town about the lameness [in her knee] you are to stay with her.' Mary was happy to send Emma advice (quite unsolicited) on various matters: 'Lady Jeune thinks you ought to see an oculist, and wear carefully chosen spectacles'. But I don't believe she ever did stay with the Jeunes in London.

Poor Emma didn't have the knack of making herself likeable. Mrs Atherton, an American, was blunt about her: 'in his wake was an excessively plain, dowdy, high-stomached woman with her hair drawn back in a little knot.... no doubt Hardy went out so constantly to be rid of her.' E.F. Benson was even ruder, describing Emma as an 'absurd, inconsequent, huffy, rambling old lady.' And when Dorothy was grown up and interviewed about her friendship with Hardy, she abandoned any pretensions to tact. 'We all hated her', she said.

Meanwhile Emma, miserable in Dorset, complained to T. P. O'Connor: 'You know, he's very vain and very selfish. And these women that he meets in London society only increase these things. They are the poison; I am the antidote.' She had a point: his weakness for interesting young women was not exactly a secret.

He may even have had a moment of romantic fancy for Mary in the early days, describing her as looking 'handsome as we sat by the fire *en tête a tête*.' But although his compliments to her sometimes exceeded the requirements of mere friendship – 'My dear friend: I am intending to arrive at your door about 5 Wednesday. Could any other woman in London have attracted me thither this weather I wonder! Remember I come to see you rather than for the dinner' – I don't believe that Mary was ever anything other than a rock on which to moor the frail craft of his emotions.

In 1893 he fell in love with Florence Henniker, and only two years later developed a passion for Mary's niece Agnes Grove. He'd been staying with Agnes' parents, Alice and Augustus Pitt-Rivers, at Rushmore in Dorset. 'It was a pleasant visit, (notwithstanding the trying temper of the hostess) – the most romantic time I have had since I visited you at Dublin', he wrote to Florence. It was not only Alice (Johnny Stanley's sister) who had a bad temper. Pitt-Rivers was famous for losing his, and the marriage was not a happy one in spite of resulting in nine children. In her diaries Agnes refers to her father as 'the Man', and to her mother as 'the minor one'.

Once she had escaped, by means of getting married, Agnes was happy enough to return home for visits, and on this occasion she was here for the annual sports day. Pitt-Rivers had created the beautiful Larmer Tree gardens on the Rushmore estate by planting woodland and building temples, pavilions, tennis courts and a bowling green. Being of a radical persuasion, he threw the gardens open to the public with no charge, and they attracted thousands of visitors every year. There were even picnic areas with thatched buildings where you could shelter in bad weather.

The sports day was held here, followed in the evening by dancing. The gardens were illuminated by thousands of Vauxhall lights, and Agnes led Hardy in the first dance. The romantic atmosphere was too much for him, and he promptly fell in love. Agnes, who by now had been married for thirteen years, did not return these feelings, although she did like Hardy advising her on her writing, which consisted of impassioned articles supporting female suffrage, and objections to vivisection and vaccination. She even went to stay at Max Gate where she got on quite well with Emma.

Hardy never forgot that night in the Larmer Tree gardens. When Agnes died of TB, years later, Hardy was still alive, and he lost no time in composing a poem for her, 'Concerning Agnes':

> I am stopped from hoping what I have hoped before —
> Yes, many a time! —
> To dance with that fair woman yet once more
> As in the prime
> Of August, when the wide-faced moon looked through
> The boughs at the faery lamps of the Larmer Avenue.

(Actually it was September, but that wouldn't have scanned.) A year after that romantic occasion they met again at her cousin Dorothy Stanley's wedding – but he didn't get to dance with her that time.

Mary was only too aware of Hardy's susceptibility to the fairer sex. She was approached by another young woman, Winifred Hope Thomson, who begged to be introduced to Hardy so that she could paint his portrait. Hardy was not that keen on sitting for portraits. He alway suspected that the artist only wanted to paint him in order to sell him the portrait afterwards. Messages passed back and forth through Mary. Winnie wrote:

> The idea that I should want him to buy it, after asking to do it makes me feel quite hot. If the portrait turns out well, and he cares to have it I should be delighted if he would accept it…

Mary passed this letter on to Hardy with a note on the back asking how she should respond. She was clearly concerned with protecting her friend, warning Hardy that Winnie is 'a *very* nice girl clever pleasant your sort but *not* pretty'. Winnie however was nothing if not persistent, following up her letter to Mary with a reminder: 'I wonder if you ever did ask Mr Thomas Hardy about being painted. Do you remember you said you would?'

And so it wasn't long before Hardy was sitting in her studio on the Gloucester Road – 'pleasant mornings' which he would look back on fondly years later. When the painting was finished Winnie was as good as her word. She gave it to Hardy, and he had it hanging at Max Gate for many years.

Hardy's addiction to love is transparently explored in his book *The Well-Beloved*, in which the hero falls serially in love with women from three generations of the same family. (In it Mary gets a cameo part, as Lady Iris Speedwell: 'the brightest hostess in London.') To Agnes he described his novel as 'more a fancy than a study of ordinary life.' Reviewers saw it differently, one writing: 'of all forms of sex-mania in fiction we have no hesitation in pronouncing the most unpleasant to be the Wessex-mania of Mr. Thomas Hardy.' This prompted another defensive letter to Mary:

> I have been much surprised & distressed by a ferocious attack in The World on my poor little book. The chief reason why I consented to republish such a slight & fantastic account of the pursuit of a Visionary Ideal was that I felt it to be at least a harmless & amusing notion, & a book which nobody could say anything against.

We don't know how Mary responded. But now her daughter Dorothy was growing up, so what was Hardy going to do?

> My dear Miss Stanley, I address you in this formal manner because there is a grown-up look about your handwriting which leads me to suspect that you have ceased to be Dorothy as she was. I will reserve my opinion on this point till I have the pleasure of seeing you.

This provoked a furious response from Dorothy, who was now

fifteen. 'I am very offended at you calling me "Miss Stanley". Please don't call me so. I can't bear it.' She ends her letter like this: 'I hope that you and Mrs Hardy are quite well. I hope you will never call me "Miss Stanley" again.'

He clearly felt the need to be circumspect, for a few years later when she was married, and still wanted Uncle Tom to accompany her to the theatre as he had done countless times before, he wrote to Emma: 'I have, of course, declined'.

Hardy wrote thousands of letters in his lifetime, and Mary features so often in them that surely, I thought, there must somewhere be letters that she wrote to him. With this in mind I made my way to the Dorset County Museum which houses various Hardy memorabilia. Had I made an appointment? the receptionist asked me (I hadn't) but some obliging volunteers offered to escort me up a narrow winding staircase to a little room under the rafters, where a number of shoe-boxes were stored on old Dexion shelving. They were labelled simply, with letters of the alphabet drawn in marker pen on the ends. The volunteers kindly opened the lid of J for Jeune – nothing. S for St Helier on the other hand struck oil, albeit only a few tiny drops…

This was my 'Who do you think you are?' moment. 'Aren't I supposed to wear gloves for this?' I asked. Apparently such refinements of the research industry had not yet reached Dorset. With great care I lifted out some letters from Dorothy (my great-grandmother) and her daughter Elizabeth. I knew that Elizabeth had died very young, at the age of 23, and that Hardy had recommended various epitaphs for her gravestone. So it was with some emotion that I read her letter thanking him for writing to her when she was ill – seven weeks in a nursing home – and signing herself 'Always yours affectionately'.

The next letter I picked up, from Dorothy, brought tears to my eyes. Still addressing him as Uncle Tom, she wrote about her son Harry who died of tuberculosis four years before Elizabeth. 'He had never known', she said, 'what it was to have a day's health'.

She adds that 'all through his many illnesses, and his frequent disappointments, I have never heard him once complain.' As for herself: 'I feel that all sunshine has gone out of my life for ever, and though it's selfish, I can't help longing to have him back.'

I was saved from having to search for a tissue by the comfortingly prosaic tone of Mary's letters. There were just two: one a note wishing Hardy a happy New Year, the second, dated 1913 and apparently in response to a query about his varicose veins, recommending that he see a specialist: 'Henry [Dorothy's husband] has been suffering from bad veins for a long time, and there is a very good man in London for veins…'

What was more interesting was a reference to a house in the country that I knew nothing about, but which she was very keen for Hardy to visit: 'So, as the maids say, Please God I am spared till next year, I think I must come and bring you forcibly to Coldash." This was to set me off on another line of enquiry, which you can read about in the Epilogue.

Mujeres Tuercas

In which Mary falls in (and out?) of love with the automobile

As I have already said, my great-great-grandmother pops up in a wide variety of unexpected places. One of the most surprising was found by my sister, who was conducting her own researches across the sea in Ireland. It was a Spanish blogsite with the title *Mujeres Tuercas*, which translates literally as 'Nuts Women'. It carries the strapline '*andá vos a lavar los platos!* (go wash the dishes!)' The author aspires to 'a world of equality, without the influence of the patriarchal society, where gender does not exist under the hood' (or bonnet if you're English). Her blog is dedicated to women who have any connection to cars or aeroplanes, including female journalists who write about them. I was particularly taken with this discovery, having been a 'nuts woman' myself for many years.

In January 2016 *Mujeres Tuercas* celebrated Mary Jeune as a 'pioneer in the art of writing about motoring'. From its author, Marily Schwander, I learned that Mary not only wrote articles about the motor car, she was one of the very first members of the Ladies Automobile Club, and took a keen interest in the latest models. Before she became a car-owner herself she took part in the inaugural cavalcade of the 1889 Motor Show, which was held at the Old Deer Park at Richmond. She and Francis and daughter Madeleine drove to Richmond from central London, in a Panhard-Levassor belonging to Alfred Harmsworth, owner of the Daily Mail. Besides the cavalcade, the motor show boasted many exhibition pavilions and jolly gymkhana events such as a slalom competition, and a 'driving backwards race'.

In 1902, following the success of her advice on what to wear whilst riding a bicycle, Mary wrote a piece on what to wear out driving. 'Dress for Ladies' was published in a book entitled *Motors and Motor-Driving*, part of the *Badminton Library of Sports and Pastimes*. A whole new vocabulary was evolving. 'Motoring – for the verb will have to be accepted and recognised – is…sufficiently near to sport to require inclusion', she said. She'd obviously decided this was a much better word than the one she'd used a year earlier, for an article in the *Gloucestershire Echo* entitled 'The Pleasures and Possibilities of Motor-Caring'. The word 'petrol' was so novel she enclosed it in quotation marks.

By now Mary had given up on her earlier-held principle that women should only practise sports which allowed them to preserve an elegant appearance. She had to admit that in an open motor car this was not possible, and she saluted the commendable lack of vanity shown by women who 'motor' (she was gathering confidence in the new verb.) The prime consideration on a journey of any length in an open motor car was keeping warm in winter, and avoiding suffocation by dust in summer. Mary's prescribed outfit for this activity consisted of a full length coat lined with chamois leather, and a tam o'shanter topped with a gauze veil in summer, or a shetland wool scarf in winter (grey so that it doesn't show the dust). The photograph that accompanied the article shows a figure with the head and face entirely swaddled, reminiscent of the Elephant Man's travelling disguise.

Mary warns that a long day on the open road does little for the complexion. I would recommend anyone who wants to save a fortune on cosmetics to follow her advice, surely harking back to her Highland childhood days, which is to start the day with cold water and a rough towel – 'and that not used sparingly,' she adds for good measure. Seven years earlier she had eulogised 'the delicious sensation one experiences in going rapidly over a good road on a light bicycle' in her *Badminton Magazine* article on 'Cycling for Women'. Now it was 'the enchanting sensation of flying along the lanes and roads of our lovely country' in a motor car.

In no time at all Mary's enthusiasm for the car resulted in her being iconised in a set of six postcards entitled 'Celebrities of the Motoring World'. These were produced by Raphael Tuck & Sons, famous purveyors of postcards, who in 1903 produced the 'Oilette' series: photographs doctored to look like oil paintings. Mary's 'Oilette' shows her in a Panhard-Levassor outside Arlington Manor with daughter Madeleine and Alfred Austin (the famously untalented poet laureate).

Whether her jaunt with Harmsworth had inspired her to buy the same make of car, or whether as his magnateship grew he sold her his at a bargain price, history doesn't relate. In any event she was in exalted company here, the other postcards in the set featuring the King, the Duke of Connaught (another Royal), Oliver Stanton, who had taught the King first to ride a bicycle, then to drive a car, and Thomas Lipton, the grocery and tea supremo, usually described in the press as the world's most eligible bachelor (journalese for 'gay'). Next Mary was invited by a certain Filson Young, one of Dorothy's

racier friends, to contribute to his comprehensive overview of all things automobile, a tome sporting the title: *The Complete Motorist: being an account of the evolution and construction of the modern motor-car, with notes on the selection, use and maintenance of the same, and on the pleasures of travel upon the public roads*. In his view, he says in the introduction, 'Lady Jeune's position in the life of our day is both unique and representative.'

Filson Young was a journalist and broadcaster distinguished more by his downright effrontery than any other claim to fame. Apparently when he was doing some research in the Royal Library at Windsor, King Edward VII came into the room and said, 'Who are you?'

'Filson Young', said Filson, 'who are you?' (Of course he knew perfectly well.)

One of Filson's sidelines was composing organ music, and when a piece of his was performed by Kendrick Pyne in Manchester he reviewed the concert for the Guardian, his chutzpah bolstered by the knowledge that his name would not appear under the piece. He skated over the programme of Bach, Handel and Mendelssohn to focus on his own composition, concluding: 'The entire work, which is of much greater value than the general run of organ compositions published at the present day, was brilliantly played by Dr Pyne and very well received by the audience.'

Filson's 1904 book on the motor car was extremely successful, going into no less than eight editions. Mary's piece in it, 'The Social Side of Motoring', started out with gusto: 'There is no sensation so enjoyable—except that of riding a good horse in a fast run—as driving in a fast motor', she declared. But she failed to maintain this sprightly tone. At the time she wrote this there were something like 23,000 cars on Britain's roads, and although motoring was still only a pastime for the rich, Mary could see a future where the car, like the bicycle, would become affordable to the general public. It did not look pretty. 'When cars can be made that will cost you £100, or even less, then we may talk of the social effect of motoring on modern life, and the effect will not, I think, be a pleasing one', she wrote, ending her piece on a forlorn note:

> There will always be a soft spot in our hearts, and a saddened memory, of the faithful horse, whose beauty it [the car] could never equal, and whose courage and willingness it could never excel. I am afraid I set out with the idea of blessing, and Alas! I have said my say.

Prophetic perhaps. These mournful sentiments didn't deter her from lashing out on a 15hp 'Noiseless Napier' a few years later. In its time the Napier was, apparently, THE car to own – provided you could afford it – until the Rolls Royce eclipsed it somewhere in the second decade of the 20th century.

Filson Young followed the success of *The Complete Motorist* with another book, *The Sands of Pleasure*. It was a novel about prostitution, condemned as immoral and therefore achieving sales in the thousands. He pursued a rackety career through two marriages and many affairs, published a book about the Titanic a month after it sank, learned to fly at 58 and at 61 passed on, he hoped, to a better place.

The Motor Car Act of 1903 raised the speed limit on public roads from 14 mph to 20, but for some this was still not fast enough. Oliver Stanton, self-styled 'Motor Expert to HM the King', appeared regularly at Marylebone Magistrate's Court on speeding offences, and even Mary had a brush with the law. She appeared at Newbury Magistrates Court, where Police-Sergeant Goddard had somehow calculated that her driver, Percival Smith, had been going at 21 miles, 1,675 yards per hour through the village of Thatcham, near Newbury, with Mary in the back.

The local newspaper recorded her impassioned defence under a banner headline: 'PEERESS' PLEA Avails Chauffeur Nothing.' In court she asserted that 'there could not be anyone more capable or careful as a driver than Smith', and she felt sure he was driving at under 20 miles an hour. They were going quite quietly through the village. She was the last person who would wish to have a car driven at a furious pace, and she felt it only just to Smith to come down from London specially to make a statement in his favour, knowing the steady and reasonable speed at which he was driving on the occasion in question. Nevertheless 'the justices, having retired and deliberated, imposed a penalty of £3, with costs, and ordered that the license should be endorsed.' Without further ado, Mary paid up.

Omdurman and After

In which Mary gives Winston Churchill a leg-up and shows her loyalty for a fallen hero

One spring evening in 1903 Mary stood on a platform at King's Cross station, just where the overnight train to Edinburgh was preparing to depart. She was not the only person there – a small crowd had gathered, some wearing highland dress, many carrying wreaths. The object of the crowd's interest lay locked in the goods van, and there was only an hour to go before the train was to leave. There was no time to waste. Mary collared the station master and insisted that he open the carriage doors, which he did, revealing to the throng a plain deal box marked with the simple legend: 'H.A.M. Edinboro'.

Everyone there knew what H.A.M. stood for: Major General Hector Archibald MacDonald, who had just committed suicide in Paris, and whose body now lay inside the box. Mary stepped forward and placed on it a bunch of red roses with a label which read: 'From his old friend, Mary Jeune.' The wagon gradually filled with flowers as, one by one, the rest of the crowd laid wreaths carrying messages such as 'For our Highland Hero' and 'Some friends whose love and faith have not failed him'. All to the accompaniment of a piper playing 'The Flowers of the Forest', a traditional Highland lament. So what had brought their hero down to this ignominious end?

This story begins in 1898, when Randolph and Jennie Churchill's son Winston approached Mary to ask a favour. He had recently returned from the Malakand province where he had been reporting on the Afghan war for the *Daily Telegraph*. Now he was desperate to go to Sudan to report on the war that had been rumbling on there for more than a decade. The trouble was that Horatio Herbert Kitchener, commander of the Egyptian forces in Sudan, hated journalists, especially 'that up-start Churchill', who had summed up the Afghan War like this: 'Financially it is ruinous. Morally it is wicked. Militarily it is an open question, and politically it is a blunder.'

Winston knew that if he could only get a commission he could still sneakily report on the action, and that Mary, with her uncanny reputation as a string-puller, was just the person to approach Kitchener for him. Actually she hardly knew Kitchener but was happy enough to send him a telegraph saying 'Hope you will take Churchill. Guarantee he won't write.' The reply came back in one syllable: 'No.'

Mary was not going to take this for an answer – she went higher up the command. It so happened that the Adjutant General, one of the most senior officers in the army and in charge of personnel, was quite a good friend of hers. Sir Evelyn Wood had spent many a weekend at Arlington Manor, and many an evening at her dinner table, where she had heard him say that Kitchener was 'going too far in picking and choosing between particular officers recommended by the War Office'. He was displeased at how the Commander in the Field appeared to be setting himself *above* the War Office – indeed he 'evinced considerable feeling upon this subject'.

A word from Mary in Sir Evelyn's ear, and within two days Winston had a commission as a supernumerary lieutenant in the 21st Lancers – as long as he understood that in the event of him being killed or wounded, 'no charge of any kind will fall on British Army funds'. In no time at all he was writing reports from the Nile for publication in the *Morning Post* under the anonymous byline 'A Young Officer'. He sent these articles, 'foundations and scaffolding' for his 1899 book *The River War*, via his mother, with a request that she show them to Mary – whether for her approval or merely for entertainment we do not know.

Even in his early twenties Winston's writing was as assured

as it was lyrical. The British and Egyptian armies were stationed just north of Omdurman, a satellite of Khartoum, and one of the hottest cities on the planet: a place, he said, where 'rainless storms dance tirelessly over the hot, crisp surface of the ground.' The climax of Winston's three-month stint in Sudan was to be the battle for Omdurman, which the Mahdists had claimed as their capital ever since they'd massacred General Gordon and his troops at Khartoum in 1885, and established an Islamic state.

The British were determined to 'liberate' Omdurman – though as Winston says, 'Never were rescuers more unwelcome.' His account of the battle of Omdurman naturally describes in great detail his own two minutes of glory, when his regiment of 400 Lancers charged a line of Sufi warriors about ten times their size. Although this cavalry charge captured the popular imagination, and spawned a rash of graphic illustrations in the press, a far greater act of heroism was enacted the same day by Colonel Hector MacDonald and his brigade of mainly Sudanese soldiers. They had somehow become separated from the rest of the British army, when they came face to face with 20,000 sword-brandishing Mahdist tribesmen.

MacDonald was not like the other officers. He came from another social class altogether, having been born into a humble stoneworker's family in the Highlands. He left school at twelve, and at seventeen absconded from a draper's apprenticeship in Dingwall to join the Gordon Highlanders as a private soldier. He then rose spectacularly through the ranks. In Afghanistan he had fought hand to hand with the enemy, saving his commander's life. This earned him promotion to second lieutenant and the nickname 'Fighting Mac'. Wherever he went, he learned the local language so that he could communicate properly with his troops; he spoke Arabic, Urdu, Hindustani, Pashto, French and Gaelic.

Now he was a Colonel, and faced with imminent slaughter by Sufi warriors, or Dervishes as the British called them. Looking down on the scene from the safety of the Surghum Hills above was *Telegraph* war reporter Bennett Burleigh, the man who had been Mary's partner in slum clearance a decade earlier. He could see MacDonald's red-coated brigade of less than 3,000 men nearly encircled by a jihadist army seven times the size, all wearing white tunics and waving flags inscribed with Koranic texts.

No doubt Burleigh's colourful description of the drama unfolding beneath him helped to seal MacDonald's subsequent status as a hero. An order to retreat was sent to MacDonald, but it came too late. From where he stood Burleigh could see that retreat would result in 'inevitable disaster to the brigade, if not a catastrophe to the army'. His *Telegraph* report included the fanciful detail that MacDonald, on receiving the order to retreat, responded in the thick highland accent that his fellow officers liked to complain was unintelligible: 'I'll no do it. I'll see them damned first! We maun just fight!' (Could Burleigh possibly have heard him from his hilltop?)

And fight they did, somewhat hampered by the extreme enthusiasm of MacDonald's Sudanese troops who fired off their muskets in all directions, wasting precious ammunition. Nevertheless the Mahdists were routed. 'I think we've given them a good dusting gentlemen' said Kitchener, who would take the credit for the victory – but there was no doubt in most minds which commander had actually won the battle.

Although a big deal was made of the relative sizes of the opposing factions, it is hardly surprising that the Brits and Egyptians came out on top. Apart from some rifles captured from previous engagements with the Egyptians, the Mahdist's weapons consisted of swords and spears. Lined up against them was that recent and most valuable asset of colonial power, the Maxim gun, the first fully automatic machine gun. Besides which, the British had gunboats on the Nile as back-up. The disparity in casualties was even greater than the difference in size of the armies: Dervishes: 11,000 dead. Kitchener's troops: 47 dead. One contemporary eyewitness noted: 'it was not a battle but an execution.'

On his return to Britain, Fighting Mac received a hero's welcome. He was made ADC to Queen Victoria – an honour that came with no pay, but on the contrary the expense of having to buy a special outfit. Bennett Burleigh, who had bonded with him over their shared Scottish background, felt that his treatment was shabby – he estimated that the 'accessories required to bedeck the person will cost at least £25.' Luckily Mary was on hand to become his patron. She had a powerful reason to support him, for as it turned out he was born at Conon Bridge, not three miles from where she herself grew up. This made him one of her own.

MacDonald was paraded through the upper echelons of British society, but no amount of attention or accolades was going to make him a happy man. Although he went on to become a Major-General, and was knighted in 1901, he would never be equal to the other officers who disdained his 'smell of the barracks'. No wonder then, that when as his final post he was sent to command the British troops in Ceylon, he preferred the company of natives to that of his snobbish colleagues. But things went badly wrong for him when rumours of homosexual activity started to surface. These became impossible to ignore when a tea-planter claimed to have surprised him *in flagrante delicto* with four Sinhalese boys in a train carriage.

MacDonald was summoned back to London to face a military tribunal. On his way he stayed in the Hotel Regina in Paris, where at breakfast he picked up an international edition of the *Herald Tribune* and saw the allegations against him splashed across the page. He went up to his room and, having stowed his jacket neatly in the wardrobe, and his boots under the bed, he blew his brains out with his pistol.

At this point, to everyone's astonishment, a wife appeared out of the blue to claim his body. He had long ago secretly married an Edinburgh school teacher many years his junior, but had kept it quiet since Kitchener did not allow his officers to marry. They had spent very little time together – only four occasions in twenty years – but had managed to produce a son, young Hector. Lady Macdonald's wish was to take her husband's body back to Edinburgh for a quiet funeral. This suited the army who naturally wanted as little fuss as possible, but they had reckoned without the fervour of the dead hero's fans, especially the Scots, who were clamouring for a funeral with full ceremonial honours. They begged Mary to go and negotiate with Lady Macdonald, and persuade her to change her mind about the funeral arrangements.

For once in her life, Mary failed: the widow dreaded the publicity and remained firm, and so in the end the box with MacDonald's body in it was transported to Edinburgh, where a discreet funeral took place at dawn in Dean Cemetery. But the following Sunday 30,000 Scots turned up to pay their respects, queuing for up to three hours to pass his grave.

Snobbery almost certainly had more to do with Fighting Mac's downfall than his sexuality. Many a heroic moustache of the era concealed a gay heart. Take General Gordon, for instance, who showed no interest in women, preferring the company of boys. His intense religious convictions may have kept him from putting his inclinations into practice, but he spent six years in Gravesend in the 1860s surrounded by 'ragged street arabs and rough sailor-lads' (according to Lytton Strachey), many of whom he took into his home for shelter. He set up schools for them, run along militaristic lines and lauded by Mary in her article 'The Children of a Great City' for *The Woman's World*. She had nothing but praise for his devotion in carrying out 'a scheme he had always keenly at heart, namely, to supply a refuge for lads between the ages of fourteen and sixteen', knowing as he did 'the dangers to a boy at such a time.' Gordon, she insisted, was a perfect model for such boys: 'deep and earnest in his convictions, temperate in his life… the embodiment of everything that was good and chivalrous in man'.

This is somewhat at odds with her personal impression of him, as recorded in her memoir. She had met Gordon at Angela Burdett-Coutts' house, where she observed 'a curiously listless-looking, nervous little man, with a sort of furtive look and expression as if he always anticipated something unpleasant.' But then as we have seen, her private opinions did not always match those expressed in her journalism.

Kitchener is also thought to have been gay, based on the rather slender evidence of his never having married, and liking to surround himself with a cadre of handsome young officers. And the fact that he collected fine porcelain and had a pet poodle. He once came to a dance that Mary gave – Francis had brought him back from a dinner at the Atheneum, and although Kitchener protested that he had never danced in his life he met his match in Mary. She insisted that he join in a quadrille known, curiously enough, as the Lancers.

Even Winston had the odd brush with homosexuality. Shortly after he graduated from Sandhurst, a fellow officer's father publicly accused him of 'acts of gross immorality of the Oscar Wilde type'. His financial and social standing were of course far superior to MacDonald's, and he was able to successfully sue his accuser, winning an apology and £500 in damages. However the allegations would continue to haunt him for a few years, thanks to the efforts of the deeply homophobic Henry Labouchère who missed no opportunity to snidely refer to them in his magazine *Truth*. For example: 'A Subaltern in a Cavalry regiment does anything that he pleases. Penalty: *nil*.' But Winston was always sympathetic to the gay fraternity, as evidenced by his close friendship with Eddie Marsh, and when he became Prime Minister by his attempts to reform the law on homosexuality – which however were blocked by right-wing back-benchers.

As for Fighting Mac, he gets no mention in Mary's memoir, for obvious reasons. The tragic irony is that he would probably have been cleared of all charges. His Court Martial further linked him to Mary, for it was prepared by the office of the Judge Advocate General – a post held at that time by none other than Sir Francis Jeune. The papers were destroyed by enemy bombers in the Second World War, but they would almost certainly have consisted of attempts to clear Macdonald's name, for it was in no-one's interest not to. As the reformist W.T. Stead had pointed out back in 1895, 'Should everyone found guilty of Oscar Wilde's crime be imprisoned there would be a very surprising emigration from Eton, Harrow, Rugby and Winchester to the jails of Pentonville and Holloway.'

Fighting Mac had a memorial erected to him in the small town of Dingwall, Easter Ross, and, appropriately enough, was further immortalised as the kilted soldier on the bottle of Camp Coffee.

Undue Influence

In which questions are asked about the power behind the scenes

Mary undoubtedly had a peculiar talent for establishing herself not only as THE authority on any subject she chose to write about, but also as the go-to person for almost anything that needed doing. If anyone needed a little help in getting on, she was the first port of call. Like a beacon planted on a rock, she radiated an aura of resolve that drew to her those who were making shipwrecks of their lives, whether through scandalous affairs or woefully inept political judgements. And as William H. Rideing pointed out

> It was her privilege to be admitted to conferences of the leaders of public opinion at which no other women were present. Her intellectual and political influence was as great as the charm which made her salon so brilliant.

It was inevitable that at some point her prestigious position would come under scrutiny.

Among those who approached her for advice were various senior politicians. From the moment she arrived in London she had made canny use of her connections, many of whom were key players in the political sphere. As C.S. Forester noted, 'half the policy of England was settled at dinner parties and social gatherings', and Mary's were no exception.

As we know, her house soon became a meeting place for politicians of diverse hues, the *Ross-shire Journal* reporting on her ability to 'lure men who never could be persuaded to enter the house of any other notable London hostess.' Her willingness to welcome persons of any political persuasion meant that the very fabric of the house was steeped in contradictory opinions, so it's not surprising that they filtered through to the nursery and schoolroom. My mother recorded Dorothy describing conflicts with her sister,

> which shattered domestic peace when they erupted into battle. 'Vote for Dizzy!' Grandma [Dorothy] would scream at Aunt Madeleine, who was already a liberal and a follower of Mr Gladstone. 'I shan't!' Madeleine would shout back. 'And then I'm afraid I pulled her across the floor by her hair,' Grandma said, 'and I told her that I wouldn't let her go until she promised to vote for Dizzy!'

Downstairs, differences of opinion were generally expressed in a more sedate fashion. Even quieter were the conspiratorial whisperings between men who otherwise only ever saw each other across the floor at Westminster. As the threat of Home Rule for Ireland loomed ever closer, Randolph Churchill began to overcome his natural distaste for his opponents, and at Mary's luncheons he was observed taking Joseph Chamberlain to one side in an uncharacteristically chummy manner.

It was not uncommon for them to be at the same table at Mary's house, but normally there would be some 'electricity in the air', if not a downright breach of the peace. Now they were colluding in an unholy alliance that would soon defeat Gladstone's Home Rule bill. For Chamberlain was an imperialist at heart, and strongly opposed to Ireland having its own Parliament. To prevent this from happening he was prepared to turn on his own leader.

Chamberlain wrote to Mary confessing that 'the position is, as you have rightly judged, a painful one for me'. (She often wrote to him over the course of his career, making useful suggestions, and he always replied – he was, she says, 'a most punctual correspondent'.)

It was no secret that Mary had the ear of the powerful, and could perhaps even influence international affairs. Ouida, writing from Italy, begged her to get Lord Rosebery (Prime Minister of the day) to take note of an article she had written for *Fortnightly Review* on the subject of Italy's tyrannical Premier, Franco Crispi, before meeting with him. 'It is so necessary', writes Ouida, 'that he should understand that no Englishman however subtle or astute can for a moment compete with an Italian in those characteristics. Crispi is a scoundrelly lawyer of the worst antecedents.' She feared that Crispi would ask Rosebery for a loan, and use it to go to war. She ends her letter by saying, 'I am sure if you were in this country yr kind and courageous heart would burn within you.' She obviously had great faith that Mary would be able to penetrate the 'crass ignorance of Italian affairs which prevails amongst English political and diplomatic men'; but whether in fact she did, history does not relate.

It is clear from other letters that many politicians used Mary as a sounding-board. A cryptic note from Charles Beresford reads: 'I want your astute opinion on a matter' – though as this was shortly before his scandalous affair with Daisy Warwick was exposed, it is just possible that he was seeking some guidance on his messy private life. Mary says that Randolph Churchill was also fond of asking advice 'of those he liked' (meaning herself) – 'which however he never followed.' Perhaps he should have listened to her more carefully when she mentioned George Goschen.

In 1886 Randolph's success in deposing Gladstone had won him the position of Chancellor of the Exchequer in the new Conservative government. He had the habit, like a naughty child, of threatening to resign whenever he wanted to get his own way; a ploy that had so far proved successful. (Prime Minister Lord Salisbury used to complain of him 'I have four departments —the Prime Minister's, the Foreign Office, the Queen and Randolph Churchill; the burden of them increases in that order'.) But when Randolph proposed defence cuts which were opposed by the Cabinet, and tendered his resignation in an attempt to force Salisbury's hand, he made an error of judgement which proved disastrous – for himself.

On hearing the news of his resignation, which she knew meant political suicide, Mary immediately summoned Randolph to the house in order to try and persuade him to change his mind. Randolph had convinced himself that he was safe because there was no-one else who could do the job, but Mary thought otherwise. 'There is Mr Goschen', she said. Randolph poured utter scorn on her suggestion, refusing to 'even consider the possibility', but within a few days George Goschen was offered the post of Chancellor, and he accepted.

At this Randolph immediately vanished abroad, possibly to escape the undiluted scorn of the press. On his return though, Mary bumped into him in Mayfair.

> About six weeks later I was driving up Brook Street when I saw him coming towards me. He stopped the carriage and shook hands, and he talked a little about various things, and then said, 'You were quite right; I forgot Goschen.'

Although this signalled the end of his political career, in Mary's version of events Randolph sounds quite calm about it. Frank Harris (unsurprisingly) gives the incident a more dramatic spin. He claims to have been told by Randolph that as soon Mary mentioned the name Goschen, 'I felt struck through the heart. I knew it was all over.' Thanks to Mary, Goschen has gone down in history as the man Randolph Churchill forgot.

At some point Mary's closeness to the most powerful people in Britain began to cause misgivings in certain quarters. When her daughter Madeleine married St John Brodrick, Conservative Secretary of State for War, and his best man was Arthur Balfour, the Prime Minister, this concern was amplified. Articles appeared in the papers openly questioning whether this gave Mary 'undue influence' at the War Office.

The Umpire newspaper, for example, claimed that it was

common knowledge that anyone who wanted to get on only had to 'ingratiate himself with Lady Jeune, and persuade that Great Lady to invite him to meet at lunch or dinner the people who can, if properly approached, obtain for him promotion or command.' It was a situation, they said, 'likely to induce the Man in the Street to imagine that the authorities at Pall Mall are more or less devotedly attached to the dainty apron strings of Lady Jeune,' and they appended a cheeky ditty:

> Each little man who wields a gun
> Must off to Harley Street quickly run
> And if he would be a general soon
> He must dance to the piping of Lady Jeune!

Vanity Fair was quick to leap to her defence. Criticism of Lady Jeune, they said, was motivated purely by jealousy. While they admitted that she was 'a power in the land', if the quickest way for a man to get to war in defence of England was to lunch or dine at her house, 'that is the fault neither of himself nor of Lady Jeune'.

It was certainly true that at Mary Jeune's table you would have a good chance of meeting one of the most senior officers in the British Army, Sir Evelyn Wood. When he was Adjutant General he had helped her to get Winston Churchill to Sudan, and now he was a Field Marshal – but to Mary perhaps more like a pet. She had to tick him off when he sat next to Joseph Chamberlain's daughter Ida, who later wrote to her stepmother that Sir Evelyn 'would whisper so many sweet nothings into my ear…that Lady Jeune was obliged to tell him he had talked to Miss Chamberlain quite long enough'. Later on Beatrice, another of Chamberlain's daughters, wrote to Neville, his son and the future Prime Minister, advising him to cosy up to Mary: 'I think she is worth cultivating & I strongly advise you to profit by her kind intentions. She always knows everybody & at her house you meet sooner or later everything worth knowing'.

As late as 1924, only three years before she was to retire from the London County Council because of age and ill health, Mary was still seen to be meddling in politics – though this probably had more to do with her adoption of Winston Churchill as a protegé many years before, and his marriage to her great-niece. In that year there was a by-election in the Westminster Abbey constituency. At the time Winston was a Liberal, but had lost his seat a couple of years earlier. He now wanted to stand as a 'Constitutionalist': a short-lived independent outfit that had arisen in response to the rise of the Labour party and the threat of Socialism.

Mary was reported to have had an interfering hand in his selection. Under the headline 'Lady St Helier Pulls the Strings', *The People* newspaper, describing her as 'a power behind the scenes in Boer War days', told the public how she had had a 'long conversation' with the existing Constitutionalist candidate, one Colonel C.W. Parkinson, in which she suggested that he should give way to Churchill.

Needless to say, Parkinson crumbled under her powers of persuasion and stood down. In fact it didn't do Winston any good, because although he went into the election with the confident expectation that he would be supported by the Liberal Unionists, in the event they decided instead to put up their own candidate, who beat him. By the end of the year he had rejoined the Conservative party, where he remained for the rest of his life.

A Great Venue for a Wedding Breakfast

In which Mary makes sure her new house is not a waste of space

After Francis' death Mary moved to no 52 Portland Place (described by John Nash as 'the most magnificent street in London'). Although both her daughters were now married and had ample properties of their own, no 52 was no less spacious than her previous two houses – in fact it was more so. It boasts an imposing frontage, with a wrought-iron balcony and doors wide enough to admit a horse and cart. Inside you can look up four storeys to a Georgian glass cupola which sheds light all down the stairwell.

What would Mary, a single woman who hated waste, want with all this space? Well, it was simple: she liked her house to be used by friends and relations for wedding celebrations, dances, meetings and the like. There were parties for grandchildren and sales of work, fundraising concerts and political discussions, a Dumb Friends' Fair and a conference on Poor Law Children. There were many meetings for the Domestic Servants Insurance Society, which she started up in 1912. A few years before her grandson Harry died of tuberculosis, she hosted a three-day conference on the illness. And so on.

Among the wedding parties held at Portland Place was one for a Mrs Lowry, who would later show Mary the bruises caused by Mr Lowry and get her to appear in court to give evidence. Another, much later on, was for the marriage of Princess Nina Georgievna, great-granddaughter of Tsar Nicholas 1 of Russia. She took as her husband Prince Paul Alexandrovich Chavchavadze, descended from the last King of Georgia, and as they had both had to leave their royal riches behind in the Soviet Union they were no doubt glad to have suitable surroundings in which to entertain their wedding guests. But the wedding breakfast that would get into the history books was that of two reluctant dinner guests, one of whom was hardly even a guest, more of an emergency stop-gap. Her name was Clementine.

Clementine Hozier was Mary's great-niece: her grandmother was Johnny Stanley's sister Blanche. She was eight years younger than her cousin Dorothy, but had lacked most of Dorothy's advantages while growing up because her parents separated when she was six, upon which her life became one of hardship. She and her sister were taken to live with their father, Henry Hozier, and his sister Mary whose discipline of choice was the whip. A spell in a strict Edinburgh boarding school was not much better, but eventually Clementine was returned to her mother – also called Blanche.

At this point her life became chaotic. Her mother's hobbies were drinking, gambling, and making friends with men – not necessarily in that order – and lack of money meant constant moves between furnished lodgings. A spell in Dieppe when she was fourteen brought her some happiness, even though her mother was busy competing with a local fishwife for Walter Sickert's attention, while her father tried (but failed) to kidnap her and bring her back to England.

Things settled down when the family moved back home and Clementine went to Berkhamstead grammar school, where she soon started to excel. However her marriage prospects were looking poor – her mother was completely ostracised for her promiscuous behaviour, and besides they had no money at all. It was time for aunt Mary St Helier to step in and save the day. Mary bought Clementine a ball gown and organised a ball for her. She had her to stay regularly, first at Harley St, then at Portland Place, so that she could meet people of brilliance and distinction.

Clearly an excellent plan, for in no time Sidney Peel, a successful barrister and banker, fell madly in love with her. He courted her for years, sending her bunches of white violets every day apart from in August, when violets were nowhere to be found. He was plainly devoted and an excellent catch, and Mary continually urged Clemmie to accept his hand in marriage – which she did, twice, but both times broke off the engagement. This was frustrating for Mary. Clemmie was now having to work for a living(!) and aged 23 she was still unattached.

One March evening in 1908 Mary held a dinner party. She had invited Flora Shaw, otherwise known as Lady Lugard, *Times* journalist and colonial expert responsible for christening Nigeria. She planned to sit Winston Churchill next to her, as he had recently been made Under-Secretary of State for the Colonial Office, so they would have plenty to talk about. A cancellation late in the day had left Mary short of a female, so she decided to send for Clementine.

At her far less fashionable address in west London, Clementine arrived home from a strenuous day's teaching to find the message from her aunt. Someone had dropped out from her dinner party that evening, and they were in danger of being thirteen at table. Could she make up the numbers? Clementine was not enthusiastic, she was tired and unprepared. However Mary had been very kind to her, and so she duly scrubbed up and made for Portland Place. There she found herself sitting next to Henry Lucy, parliamentary commentator and friend of Ernest Shackleton, who would name a mountain in Antarctica after him the following year. A man in his sixties, even older than aunt Mary, he was perhaps not the most stimulating companion – according to Frank Harris 'He met everyone, and knew no-one'. On Clementine's other side was an empty chair.

Winston meanwhile had been lying in his bath in Mayfair, grumbling about the dinner party that he was supposed to attend, and which he thought would be a bore. Eddie Marsh, Winston's private secretary and lifelong friend, reminded him gently of the favour that the hostess had done him ten years earlier when he was twenty-three and desperate to get to Sudan. Duty called. Reluctantly he got out of his bath, put on his dinner jacket and set off for Portland Place.

When he arrived, rather out of breath, the diners were already on the chicken course. He fell into the only empty seat and turned straight away to Clemmie: 'Have you read my book?' he said. (His biography of his father Randolph had just been published.) Despite this graceless opening gambit, he held Clemmie's attention for the rest of the meal. Flora Shaw, on his other side, was none too pleased at being ignored. When it was time for the gentlemen to join the ladies Winston could not get out of the room fast enough, and he continued to be engrossed in Clemmie for the rest of the evening.

In fact Clemmie had met Winston some three years earlier, but had been deeply unimpressed – he had just stood and stared at her awkwardly. Besides, someone had told her that he was bumptious and insufferable. This evening was different: now she found him charming and brilliant, and the following month she went to spend a weekend with him and his mother Jennie (recently remarried to a Scots Guards officer two weeks younger than Winston). The visit confirmed their feelings, but immediately afterwards Clemmie and her mother set off for Germany to collect her sister Nellie, who was recovering from tuberculosis. Mary told Blanche that she must be mad to remove Clemmie from the scene just as Winston was getting interested.

Their return was followed by a couple of months of tense waiting, until in August Winston invited Clemmie to stay at Blenheim. He proposed to her in a Greek temple overlooking the lake, and she accepted. As he was strongly opposed to a long engagement, there followed a hectic rush to organise a wedding the following month.

The Hozier house in Kensington was very small, so naturally Mary offered her house for the reception. Clemmie moved into 52 Portland Place the night before the wedding, in order to make room for other family members in her mother's house. On the actual morning of the wedding however, Clemmie had a bad attack of cold feet. According to her daughter, Mary Soames,

> On the spur of the moment she decided to go home for breakfast; but this was easier wished than done, as all her everyday clothes had been swept away the night before by her great-aunt's lady's maid. In her dressing gown she crept downstairs: the great rooms were still in darkness, but in the morning room a young under-housemaid was busily blacking the grate. Clementine confided to her the great longing she had to go home... the friendly girl ran upstairs and returned with a complete set of her own best 'going out' clothes. Shortly afterwards Clementine was let out of the back door, attired in a pretty print dress, dark close-fitting coat and black-buttoned boots, with a neat bonnet and kid gloves. The early buses were running, and she caught one on the route she often used. As he gave her a ticket, the conductor eyed her narrowly. 'Ain't you going the wrong way, Miss?' he said.

Her arrival at Abingdon Villas in the maid's clothes was greeted with some astonishment. But once a cheerful breakfast with her family had restored her courage, Clemmie went back to Portland Place in time to get ready for the wedding, without aunt Mary even realising she had absconded. 1300 guests turned up for the occasion at St Margaret's, Westminster, and the man who took Clementine up the aisle was not Henry Hozier but Bertie Mitford, grandfather of the famous Mitford sisters. He was Clemmie's uncle – but believed also to be her biological father. Out on the streets vast crowds waved as the couple made their way to Portland Place, because Winston was already a popular figure. Only Mary was a little late for her own party, her brougham colliding with a motor car on the way home.

Photographs of the wedding breakfast were taken by John William Righton, a popular recorder of society events, but they have all since disappeared. In order to picture the setting for this occasion I paid a visit to no 52 Portland Place, now in the hands of a property developer by the name of David Coffer. He was more than welcoming, inviting me to take a look around the building.

To my surprise the first floor reception rooms had been carefully preserved much as they were in Mary's day. They were full of Churchill memorabilia – Coffer explained to me that he was a great fan of the Churchills, and that he owned another property by Regent's Park that had also belonged to the family. I explained back at him that it was Mary I was more interested in than the Churchills, at which he murmured, as he showed me out, that sometimes when he was alone there in the evening he *felt her presence*. This couldn't have been more satisfactory, and I left with a smile on my face.

Clemmie was close to her cousin Dorothy, and the Churchills often stayed with her at Stoke Poges. Indeed, Clemmie spent the last few weeks of her first pregnancy there, playing with her young cousins Madeleine (my grandmother) who was twelve, and Harry and Elizabeth who were ten and seven. I couldn't help but be struck by the couple's signatures in Dorothy's visitor's book: Clementine's is nearly twice the size of Winston's.

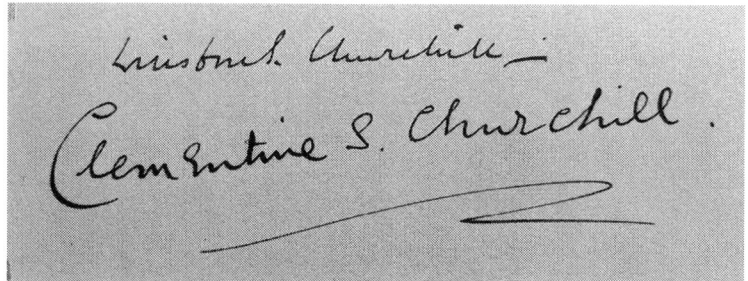

Widowhood and Work

In which Mary shows that there's no need to be useless just because you're a Lady

Francis Jeune died at the age of 56, a couple of months after being raised to the peerage. He had never been very strong physically, and had worked hard all his life. Perhaps the busy social life that was inflicted on him at evenings and weekends had taken its toll. I think that others may have commented on this, for I found this defensive passage in Mary's memoir:

> There is a division of opinion as to whether a very busy man is not overtaxed by the claims of social life added to his work, but I have always found that the relaxation which society affords to those undergoing a severe course of mental work has a beneficial, and not injurious effect.

I couldn't help but think of Lady Bracknell telling Algernon that 'Health is the primary duty of life. I am always telling that to your poor uncle, but he never seems to take much notice…'

The early death of their son was the straw that broke the camel's back. Francis went into a rapid decline, dying less than a year later. He was buried next to Francis junior in Chieveley churchyard, near Arlington Manor, under a stone bearing an inscription composed by Mary: 'In grateful remembrance of his love and sweet companionship during twenty three years of the greatest happiness.' She was now Lady St Helier; she more or less stopped writing for the periodical press and sold Arlington Manor.

The *Tatler* reported that she had taken a house in 'unlovely Shoreditch, where she spends the greater part of her time attending to the direction of many charitable and philanthropic undertakings.' This was not quite accurate. In fact the Shoreditch house was just a temporary arrangement, possibly owing to probate difficulties. It seems that the eminent lawyer, having fallen out with his brother, had altered his will in a most unorthodox way: he had torn out a couple of pages. Mary, in deep mourning garb, had to appear in court. Luckily the judge pronounced in favour of the will, but rather crossly said he thought that 'Lord St Helier would be the last person in the world not to leave his will in a proper condition.'

If in the eyes of her public Mary was retiring from society, much as Queen Victoria had done on the death of Prince Albert, this was far from being the case. Not being one for radical change in her domestic circumstances, she moved very slightly eastwards, from Harley Street to Portland Place. By now the Portland estate had become the Howard de Walden estate, which to this day maintains ownership of 850 buildings in Marylebone.

The days of crushes may have been over, but there would be plenty going on in the new house. Nor did she lay down her pen – she set to work on writing her memoir instead. When it was published, *Memories of Fifty Years* flew off the shelves, going into three editions in the first year. According to the *Votes for Women* newspaper, the Times Book Club had to insert 'a pathetic little slip beseeching the reader to send back the volume at the earliest possible moment,' demand from women readers being so great. This is quite surprising considering that Mary's record of her life was facing stiff competition in the same year (1909) from *My Recollections*, the ghost-written autobiography of Lady Adeline de Horsey Cardigan, whose life was one long string of outrageous scandals. And that the *Tatler* described Mary's book as 'a rather dull but most respectable book of memoirs.' Two years later the same Times Book Club was offering it at a sale price of 2/6d, marked down from 15 shillings.

Henry Lucy found her book 'provokingly discreet', and could not resist leaking a couple of dinner party anecdotes that Mary had not seen fit to include. One, already quoted, was about Henry Labouchère and his concubine-turned-wife; the other concerned the best-selling novelist Ouida. Apparently, although her romances were stuffed with earls, duchesses and countesses, Ouida had never actually met a real live duchess. Mary, 'kindest, most good-natured of women, arranged to fill up this deplorable gap' by inviting a well-known duchess to dine with her. Unfortunately, Her Grace had to cancel at the last moment. Ouida sat through the meal 'in a state of stony frigidity, not to be thawed by the winning manner of her hostess or the attentions of the company, which at least included one Baron of the United Kingdom, and a KCB'.

Mary was now stepping up her work in social reform. She was a member of the London County Council's education committee, managing schools and day nurseries and dealing with infringements of the Employment of Children Act. In 1908 she was asked to give evidence to a House of Commons select committee on Infant Life Protection. They were proposing to send government inspectors into foster homes, which might sound like a sensible idea – Mary, however, was strongly opposed to it, and for very good reasons.

Standing in front of the committee, Mary outlined her twenty-five years' experience of helping single mothers to find childcare so that they could go back to work. Something like 1,400 of these women had passed through her hands, and she had kept in touch with many of them. She told the examiners why their scheme would be disastrous. She knew exactly what people thought of government inspectors, and as usual she did not mince her words. The committee recorded her evidence verbatim:

> There is the very greatest dislike and distrust among the working classes in England of anything like inspection… they do not like anybody who is an official, they hate the tax collector, and they hate anybody who comes as a Government official and tries to go into their houses. I know from my own experience that many of these husbands will say to their wives: 'You shall not take a child

now; if I am to have an Inspector coming into the house you shall not take a child'.

This, she pointed out, was sure to make less childcare places available, and those that were available more expensive. She continued:

> What I am so afraid of is that if these single homes are done away with we shall have these girls saying 'I cannot afford to pay this money; I have no place to go to, I have nobody to turn to; what am I to do?' And the girl may either destroy herself or the child. I do not quite see what these girls are to do, because so few of them get any support from the father of their child.

At this point her interlocutor became slightly uncomfortable, saying 'Need you elaborate this? We are men of the world...' To which she answered firmly, 'I must put what I feel so strongly about, and I will not say more than is necessary.' She concluded her evidence with these words: 'I say if this is done, you will not have the children taken at all, and what is a woman to do?' Her vehemence was not lost on the committee, who concluded that foster households should be exempt from inspection where appropriate, and that if an inspection did take place it should be 'deprived of any rigid, formal or official character.'

This was all serious stuff, but it should not be thought that Mary was having no fun. In 1911 she and her sister Julia attended a private production of Wilde's *Salome*, which had been banned on grounds of blasphemy and was not performed publicly in England until after Mary's death. She was also becoming something of a gay icon, befriended by a coterie of writers she met at her daughter Dorothy's. These included Somerset Maugham and E.F. Benson, who shared the rent of a holiday property in Capri (where sodomy was not illegal).

Benson was the product of a family apparently devoid of

heterosexual DNA: his mother was constantly passionately in love with other women, while his father's sexuality was strictly concealed behind the dual facades of stern paterfamilias and Archbishop of Canterbury. Mary I think must have penetrated his disguise, judging by a sly comment in her memoir about 'that most saintly and holy-looking Archbishop – for surely no man ever impersonated his office better than Dr. Benson.' Edward Benson junior refers to Mary in many glowing terms.

Even closer to her was H.H. Munro, better known as Saki. His cousin Dornford Yates (another writer) reported that 'he was much liked by Lady St Helier – a widow, old enough to be his mother – and frequently visited her at her country house.' She was clearly the model for Dowager Lady Greymarten in Saki's futuristic, and sadly rather dull, novel *When William Came:*

> She had worked and schemed and fought with an energy and far-sightedness that came probably from the blend of caution and bold restlessness in her Scottish blood... In her town house or down at Torywood, with her writing-pad on her knee and the telephone at her elbow, or in personal counsel with some trusted colleague or persuasive argument with a halting adherent or half-convinced opponent, she had laboured on behalf of the poor and the ill-equipped... not least of her achievements, though perhaps she hardly realised it, was the force of her example, a lone, indomitable fighter calling to the half-caring and the half-discouraged, to the laggard and the slow-moving.

Evidence that Saki was gay is limited to his frequent references to pretty boys and 'clean-limbed menservants', and to the fact that after his death on the Somme his sister Ethel destroyed all his correspondence, leaving a thankless task for his biographers.

In 1910, at the age of 65, Mary was the first woman to be elected as an alderman to the London County Council. The *Illustrated*

London News did wonder whether she shouldn't be an 'alderwoman', but said they would leave it up to her: 'It is a point Lady St Helier herself must decide, for she has caused a case for which there is no precedent, unless it be that Dr Garrett Anderson is called Mayor, and not Mayoress, of Aldeburgh.'

In this work, as in everything she did, she was extremely conscientious. She attended the LCC assiduously for seventeen years, until old age and illness made it impossible for her to continue. On one occasion she sat through a meeting that lasted from 2.30 in the afternoon until ten to eight the following morning, earning praise in the papers next day for her endurance and 'remarkable devotion'.

Time spent at the LCC did not stop her from keeping her hand on the wheel of the many good causes she'd started up in the previous century, such as the Children's Happy Evenings Association, which ran after-school clubs in the East End, and a charity that provided Christmas stockings, which had earned her the sobriquet 'Lady Santa Claus'. The Happy Evenings Association had been the object of some derision when she started it. Once it was working well Mary invited one of its most cynical critics to come and see for herself, saying in a rather Wildean way, 'Dear friend, nothing worth doing is ever accomplished without ridicule.'

Another successful venture was the Poor Children's Boot Fund, which by 1907 was distributing 26 thousand pairs of boots. Apparently not everyone thought the Boot Fund a good use of money, in particular this Scotsman who wrote to the *Times*:

> May I suggest to the Chairman of the London County Council, to Lady St Helier, and to other charitable people that the poor childrens Boot Fund is altogether superfluous? Let the London children follow the wise example of their Scottish cousins and discard bothe shoes and socks altogether. They will then come to school with sound and healthy soles, will not pass any part of the day with soddened feet, and will never catch cold. Their feet will always be warm, healthy, and comfortable, a dry rub when they

reach school on a wet day being all that is necessary. The £2,828 13s and 9d would have been more profitable expended in lining their stomachs than in covering their skins.

The Scot in Mary might have had some sympathy with his view. She was certainly a firm believer in the benefits of fresh air, and to this end she had helped to set up organisations that took urban dwellers out into the countryside: the Children's Holiday Fund and the Factory Girls Holiday Fund.

She had even helped Joseph Merrick to find somewhere to enjoy nature and escape prying eyes. Merrick is better known as the Elephant Man, the title under which he was displayed in a travelling freak show. Mary's neighbour in Wimpole Street, the surgeon Frederick Treves, had rescued Merrick and raised funds for him to be lodged in the London Hospital where he soon became a celebrity, attracting the friendship of society ladies. They liked to bring him gifts – Dorothy Nevill, for example, gave him a silver watch – but Mary's was of a more practical nature. A report of his case in the British Medical Journal makes special mention of 'the Hon Mrs Jeune, to whom he indirectly owes his country holiday' – presumably through her friendship with Lady Knightley of Fawsley, who allowed Merrick to stay on her estate.

Mary was also keen on open air schools, which were being introduced as an effective way of controlling tuberculosis. In 1914 she wrote an introduction to a book on the subject, in which, as is so often the case, she is careful to let you know that she is an authority on the subject.

> Only those [i.e. herself] who have seen the puny, undersized, anaemic boys and girls on their entry into the School, and revisited it after a few months, can realise what Open Air Schools have done and will do in the future...

At the LCC Mary worked on the Education Committee,

putting pressure on the authorities to take on the job of feeding schoolchildren, preferably for free, a battle which continues to this day. As may be imagined, she was a robust contributor to council debates. When 500 London schoolchildren were invited by the Paris Municipal Council to attend a three-day music festival in Paris, she objected; she desired, she said

> to oppose nothing that would preserve the entente cordiale; but they knew what the state of the traffic on steamers and also on railways, both in France and England, was at Whitsuntide. At the Gare du Nord it was indescribable; Derby Day was absolute quiet compared with it...

Because the committee was intent on accepting the invitation she eventually agreed to withdraw her objection – but could not resist 'remarking at the same time that she had not altered her opinion.'

Away from the council chamber she did not relax. It had come to her attention that the first National Insurance Act, in 1911, excluded domestic servants from such benefits as sickness and unemployment pay. So in July of 1912 she decided to set up an independent Domestic Servants' Insurance Company. This was more successful than she could have imagined, attracting over 19,000 applications in the first month, and boasting 24,000 members by September. She held meetings at her house and carried representations from them to the LCC. In 1920 the Act was finally extended to cover domestic staff.

Mary's work did not go unnoticed, and in 1920 she was honoured with an OBE, followed in 1925 by a DBE (or to give its full name, 'Dame Commander of the Order of the British Empire'). Overleaf you can see her leaving Buckingham Palace waving the paperwork, accompanied by my grandmother Madeleine.

Mary continued to campaign for better housing for working

people. In 1925 she put her name to a manifesto which detailed obstacles to speedy slum clearance. Nothing much had changed, it seemed, since the 1880s when she had launched her first swipe at bad housing conditions, and she blamed 'the cumbersome and dilatory procedure involved in the acquisition by local authorities of insanitary property.' It was still taking an average of at least eight years from ordering clearance of a slum to the completion of new dwellings.

Mary was enthused by the garden city movement, and held a meeting at Portland Place to raise funds for a school in Hampstead Garden Suburb. However her days of agitating for decent housing were nearly at an end. At the age of 82 illness forced her to stand down from the LCC. The *Illustrated London News* noted her resignation: 'To most Londoners of the present day, Lady St Helier is known as the slender and alert lady dressed rather severely in black who has been a prominent and active member of London County Council for more than sixteen years'.

The previous year the LCC had made a compulsory purchase of over 800 acres of lavender fields in Mitcham, south London, where they planned to build a new council estate, and to honour Mary's years of service by naming it St Helier. The inhabitants of St Helier in Jersey were not entirely happy about this, suggesting 'Jeuneville' as a possible alternative, but that was ignored.

The St Helier council estate was designed along the principles of a garden suburb, with houses grouped around green open spaces, and mature trees preserved. If you go there today you might feel that the time has come to delete the word 'garden'. St Helier Avenue, the sweeping boulevard which dissects it, is better known as the A297, home to several bus routes and some of the worst traffic congestion in London.

But for families who relocated in the thirties it was like heaven. Many had moved from a couple of rooms with an outside lavatory, cooking facilities on the staircase shared with several other families, and a candle to light you to bed. Here you had your own front door, lighting at the flick of a switch, and views of grass and trees from the windows. As one resident remarked: 'Everything seemed so bright and new and happy.' Mary never saw the new railway station, the hospital, or the pub, all of which bore her name, as sadly she did not live to see the project completed.

The Meteoric Career of Billy Bishop

In which Mary 'adopts' a Canadian airman and helps him to cheat his way to the top

If Mary's work at the LCC kept her busy, she must have been working overtime once the Great War broke out. She became very involved with the setting up and running of military hospitals, and it was in one of these that she came across a young man whose life she would change in a most dramatic fashion.

Before that however, on June 30th 1914, between the shooting of Archduke Ferdinand and the declaration of war on Germany, Mary just had time to fit in a big luncheon party at Portland Place. D.H. Lawrence was there with Frieda. She had first invited him in February – a sure sign that he had 'arrived' – but then he was in Italy and unable to come. He had written:

> Dear Madam, I am sorry that I am too far away to accept your invitation to lunch. I feel so embedded in this lazy little bay that an invitation to Portland Place quite scares me, it feels so strenuous. I think I shall be in London for 3 or 4 months of the summer. If ever you should remember to ask me again, during that time, I shall be very pleased to come... Forgive me if I don't know how to address you fittingly.

Lawrence appears both cowed and flattered by the invitation, but Frieda did *not* like society luncheons: 'You were fed more or less well, you sat next to somebody whose name had also been printed in the papers, the hostess didn't know who or what you were...' It is only fair to say that Mary was less revered by the modernists than she had been by the Victorians. When she died, in 1931, Virginia

Woolf noted in her diary: 'Death of Lady St Helier – who was so d--d condescending to me, 30 years ago.' But then Woolf was inclined to be snippy: she condemned both Lawrence and Joyce as the most overrated English writers of their time.

As soon as the War was in full flow Mary got down to the important business of making sure that the local military hospitals were up to standard. She was in charge of furnishing a home for wounded Belgian Soldiers at Ewell Grove, and a hospital in Bryanston Square for aviators. She also organised entertainments and worked as an almoner at the County of London War Hospital near Epsom.

The soldiers adored her – one said he would never forget 'the little lady who visited us, armed with a large basket of cigarettes, packs of cards, stationery, and novels. We worshipped the ground on which she walked.' The programme of entertainments at Epsom was impressive: in 1916 the *Mirror* reported that the hospital boasted 'on an average, six concerts per week. In addition there are billiard matches, lectures on the war, and even three-act plays, so they are not neglected, these soldier men.'

Mary's other work there, as almoner, was what today would be done by a medical social worker. She was responsible for setting up after-care for patients: stays in convalescent homes, special equipment for use at home, extra nutritional needs and so on. A Mrs E.A. Thomson of Epsom who had worked at the hospital sent this story to the paper:

> An Irish-born London navvy serving with the Middlesex Regiment was brought to the hospital among a convoy of wounded, and Lady St Helier learned from him that his wife had just had their third baby. In consequence they were badly off, etc, etc. She told him not to worry, and the wherewithal for the wife to visit her husband and to pay for rooms in the district was forthcoming.
>
> The man, only slightly wounded, soon recovered, and within a year was again in the hospital. Thinking Lady St Helier would

not remember him, and knowing her kind heart, he had his tale ready. In she came with her note-book to take down particulars of his case. All was going well until she asked 'How many children, Murphy?'

'Seven, yer ladyship!'

'Seven, Murphy? How can that be? When you were here ten months ago you had only three.'

'Only three, yer ladyship?' said Murphy, seeing the game was up. 'Indeed, yer ladyship, then I must have misnumbered them, but it's my mistake entirely.'

Murphy did not get helped that time.

Mary's prodigious memory for people was about to wreak an epic change in one young man's life. The hospital at 37 Bryanston Square was in a house lent by a Lady Tredegar for use by the Royal Flying Corps, and Mary had contributed beds and equipment. It was on a visit here in May 1916 that she came upon a young Canadian with a badly injured knee. She recognised the name on his bed, William Avery Bishop. She had had a brief acquaintance with his father, also William Bishop, in Canada some years before. Apparently she decided on the spot to take young Billy under her wing, and offer him 'lodgings' at Portland Place.

Billy Bishop had long nursed an ambition to be a pilot. When he was 15 years old he made his first attempt at flight, in an aircraft he had constructed himself from cardboard, an orange crate, and 'much strong string.' He launched it down the sloping roof of his family's house in Owen Sound, Ontario, and somehow managed to escape serious injury in spite of demolishing the plane. This set a firm precedent – landing never was to be his strong point, and in time he would destroy many more planes as he hit the ground.

At the age of seventeen he enrolled in the Royal Military College of Canada, but he was not a good student. The 'worst cadet RMC ever had' ended his three year stint there by handing in his crib notes with his exam papers – he couldn't even cheat successfully. However he was a brilliant shot, which earned him a post in the 7th Canadian Mounted Rifles.

In 1915 he was sent to the front in France. In his autobiography he recalls staring up at the sky from the bottom of a trench and resolving to become a pilot. 'It's clean up there' he told himself. 'I'll bet you don't get any mud or horse shit on you up there, and if you die at least it would be a clean death.' He duly managed to get transferred to the Royal Flying Corps, but there were no vacancies for pilots and he had to fly as a mere observer, on reconnaissance and bombing flights.

Flying was still in its infancy. The Wright brothers had made the first powered flight in 1903, and the RFC was only established in 1912. Planes were hardly more sophisticated than Billy's orange-box creation: bombs were dropped by hand over the side, and you could never be sure that your parachute would open when needed.

After surviving a number of minor accidents, Billy came to London on leave. While disembarking at Folkestone full of celebration champagne, he slipped and hurt an already injured knee, and ended up in hospital. What happened next was recounted in the somewhat fanciful biography written by Billy's son, William Arthur Bishop: *The Courage of the Early Morning*.

> He awoke from a drugged sleep and found himself gazing into the eyes of a woman who was bending over him. She was old and lean, with sparse hair severely drawn back to show unusually large ears. Her most remarkable features were her wide-set luminous eyes that appeared much younger than the rest of her, eyes that penetrated and probed and yet were kindly and reassuring. Bishop had met one of the three most important women in his life.

What followed was something of a fairy tale for Billy. Mary took him back to stay at Portland Place, then arranged with his superiors for him to go back to Canada for some home leave. This was quickly granted, with the result that he missed the battle of the Somme in which most of his aptly-named Suicide Squadron were wiped out.

On his return to London in September he applied again for active duty, but was turned down. A medical examination pronounced him unfit for active service, and anyway his service records had gone missing, so he could not apply for pilot's training. His one ambition was being frustrated, and there was nothing he could do about it. Mary, however, could. She got on the phone to Winston Churchill, and Churchill's best man, Lord Hugh Cecil, who was Secretary for Air. A few days later Billy was summoned to the War Office. According to his son Arthur,

> Stiff formality was swept aside. Bureaucratic procedure became friendly cooperation. The brick walls of English protocol suddenly developed open arms. My papers appeared from nowhere.

A cursory medical exam declared him fit to fly, and at last he was a pilot.

Billy was prone to air-sickness and accidents of all kinds, one of his comrades in 60 Squadron describing him as 'a fantastic shot but a terrible pilot'. He never could get the knack of landing, possibly damaging more allied planes than he did German ones. But he was completely fearless, and started racking up prodigious scores against the enemy. By the end of the year he had also racked up a Military Cross, a DSO, and a Victoria Cross. Soon after he added a Distinguished Flying Cross, a Chevalier of the Legion of Honour, and a Croix de Guerre. He became such a national hero in Canada

A typical Billy Bishop landing

that by June 1918 he had to be grounded, because they could not risk the detriment to national morale that would result if he 'went west'.

All these military honours were good for business. The fact that many of Billy's bullseyes were uncorroborated was an inconvenient truth, and passed over. His VC was one of only two that were ever awarded for an action that had not been witnessed, and German records – which are meticulous – fail to substantiate many of the claims he made about shooting down their planes, especially in his last year of flying. His reputation for exaggeration and manipulation, and his habit of undertaking 'lone wolf' attacks, fuelled scepticism in several quarters. Lord Hugh Cecil, who had appointed Billy in the first place, said to him: 'You've done rather well, I hear. You know, I wasn't at all sure you were the type.'

At Mary's, however, he could do no wrong. She bought him a 'glorious' flying coat for £25 (seen in this picture), and introduced him to all her friends. At dinner at Portland Place he sat next to Princess Marie Louise, lively divorcée daughter of Princess Christian and first cousin to King George V. Billy wrote to his fiancée Margaret:

> I made a great hit. Under the influence of champagne I told her the most brilliant lie of my career. I told her Louie [his sister] was named after her, which so pleased her that Lady St Helier has today received an order to bring me to see her father, old Prince Christian.

Mary wrote to Billy's mother with pride:

> Princess Marie Louise told me last week that the King said the *one* thing he wanted was to give the VC, DSO, and MC, at the same time... and now Billy is the first person who has won them all and the King is very pleased as he has heard so much about him from the Princess.

Her protegé had excelled even her expectations. According to his son Arthur's less than impartial biography,

> A strong bond of affection had grown between the young Canadian country boy and one of Britain's most sophisticated noblewomen... in a rare sentimental moment this indomitable woman told Bishop 'You are the kind of grandson my son would have given me if he had lived'. Her voice was choked. She was close to tears. It was the first time Bishop had seen her show anything but cheerfulness and self assurance. He tried to comfort her in the only way he knew by saying with an impertinent grin: 'Yes, Granny.' From then on he called her Granny.

It is hard not to feel a little sceptical of this account. Certainly John Maclachlan Gray, author of the musical play *Billy Bishop Goes to War*, had his doubts, as can be seen from this excerpt:

> BISHOP: Good morning, Granny.
> LADY ST. H: Bishop! Sit down. I have a bone to pick with you. Cedric, the colonial is under the weather. Bring tea and Epsom salts. Where were you last night, Bishop?
> BISHOP: I was out.
> LADY ST. H: Good. Very specific. Well, I have my own sources and the picture that was painted for me is not fit for public viewing. Disgusting, unmannered and informal practices in company which is unworthy even of you, Bishop. But what

concerns me is not where you were, but where you were not. To wit, you were not at a party which I personally arranged, at which you were to meet Bonar Law, Chancellor of the Exchequer. What do you have to say in your defence?
BISHOP: Look, Granny...
LADY ST. H: I'll thank you not to call me Granny. The quaintness quite turns my stomach.'

To me this sounds more authentic. In any case Mary had a perfectly good grandson of her own, Dorothy's son Harry Allhusen, by now seventeen and due to go to Trinity College Cambridge.

Billy Bishop goes to War became one of the most famous and widely shown plays in Canadian theatre. It was a two-hander, with Gray playing the piano while Eric Peterson played all the parts, including that of Lady St Helier and her butler Cedric. It toured its homeland many times, and was staged in Washington DC, on and off Broadway, at the Edinburgh Festival, in Los Angeles and London and Frinton on Sea. It was revived in Ottawa in 2009 and in Toronto in 2017. It won the Los Angeles Drama Critics' Award, the Floyd S. Chalmers Canadian Play Award, and the Governor General's Award for English Drama.

Opinion as to whether Billy was all he's cracked up to be remains divided, but Toronto's City Airport wears his name with pride. And although his son Arthur's *Courage of the Early Morning* may have sacrificed some accuracy for the sake of colour, it does offer a convincing picture of Mary in her natural habitat:

> Lady St Helier was sitting at an antique desk, writing letters. She had a unique method of turning out her correspondence. As each letter was finished she tossed it to the floor. From time to time a footman entered the room, gathered the scattered sheets and put them into the appropriate envelopes. Bishop never tired of watching this strange performance. Granny had explained that she evolved this system because her desk was so cluttered with

letters, cards, invitations, London County Council reports and other assorted paper-work of an incredibly busy life that there was no room on her desk for her own letters.

Billy kept up his friendship with Princess Marie Louise and introduced his team of pilots to her. The 'colonials' – American and Canadian airmen – understandably did not have a clear idea of royal protocol, and were inclined to be rather informal – not that she appeared to mind. Her mother was perhaps more old-fashioned. Shortly after the war Mary invited some Canadian officers to dinner with Princess Christian at Portland Place. Also present was a journalist who recorded this instance of Mary bringing 'social tact up to the point of high art.'

> The officers were much exercised regarding deportment.
> 'What shall we call the Princess?' they asked.
> 'Call her "Your Highness" first,' said Lady St Helier, 'and then call her simply 'Ma'am'. Also, it would be better to let her start any subject of conversation.' All went well for a time – but Lady St Helier's claret was notoriously good, and the officers, finding, I fear, that the Princess' conversational openings were not too lively, began to talk a good deal among themselves, neglecting her.
> Suddenly the Princess leaned forward and said, with devastating chillness:
> 'What a terrible thing you have done in letting my cousin Nicky be so foully murdered.' In the appalled silence that followed one officer alone was bold enough to say, 'Do you mean the Czar?'
> 'Yes,' said the Princess.
> 'Well,' said the officer, 'I guess the job was too big for him anyway.'
> It is difficult to know how a lesser hostess would have coped with this situation. Lady St Helier simply said: 'My dear, I do so want you to see my miniatures.'

Epilogue

In which I come across an unexpected connection in a Berkshire village

On a cold day in January 2019 I drove down to Berkshire in pursuit, I hoped, of some final details of Mary's life. I had arranged to meet up with William A. Davis, an American academic whose name had cropped up with great regularity in the early days of my internet research. He turned out to be one of Mary Jeune's most faithful fans, having lectured on her journalism for 25 years as part of his Victorian literature course at Notre Dame university in Maryland. He was the author of several papers on her journalism, none of which I could read online as I wasn't attached to an academic institution. When I wrote to him he was delighted to make contact with one of Mary's descendants, and as he was about to retire he sent me hard copies not only of his own essays, but nearly all of hers, packed up in an impressively bulky envelope.

Bill (as I now know him) was in the habit of coming to England every year with a group of students, and taking them to such salubrious heritage sites as Bath, Salisbury and Stonehenge. Today we had planned to go to the village of Cold Ash, not far from Thatcham station where I picked him up. Before doing that, however, we drove to the Jeune country house, Arlington Manor, which today is the Mary Hare School for deaf children, a repurposing that Mary would have thoroughly approved. Bill had brought a gift for the Principal, a copy of *Memories of Fifty Years*. When we'd had a look round we drove on to Cold Ash.

After I'd come across Mary's mention of a house in 'Coldash' in her letter to Thomas Hardy, I did some detective work. Online I found an image of a property in the village called St Helier, which sounded promising – but it was far too new, a boxy little house built in the twenty-first century. Eventually I tracked down a reference to Mary having a house built for her, by the name of Poplar Farm, but when I looked that up it turned out to be a Grade 2 listed building dating from 1622. I was confused. However there was a website attached to that address because it was the home of a business called Celebration Carriages, and it made mention of a diary kept by the grandfather of the current owner. I sent him an email.

Over the course of a few more emails, a proper picture emerged. Mary bought Poplar Farm at auction in 1905, immediately after selling Arlington Manor. In those days Cold Ash had a population of around 800 people, with four pubs, a post office and bakery, two shoe repairers and a smithy, and a variety of other workshops, mostly long since gone. Few people travelled outside the village for work.

Today its population is more than 3000, and the busy road that runs north/south through the middle has protruding barriers designed to slow the traffic. Poplar Farm came with 70 or so acres attached, but Mary clearly decided that the old farmhouse was not big enough. She had a new house built just up the road, commanding nice views to the south-west over her farmland, and called it Poplar Farm House.

When the new house was completed she let the original one to a farmer called Alfred Collins, and he bought it off her in 1921. The mystery of the brand new house called St Helier was solved: it was built on a patch of land that Mary had donated to Cold Ash for the building of a Parish Room. This structure, of timber and corrugated iron, was put up by the men of the village but was eventually superseded by a new Parish Room attached to the church. No doubt the Parish got a good price for the land owing to its proximity to Thatcham station, a handy commuter link to London.

Alfred Collins' grandson Clive was now running the farm and Celebration Carriages, and after consulting with his siblings he said it would be all right for me to look at his grandfather's diary. So I made an appointment to go and visit him at Poplar Farm, and Bill Davis was keen to come along. When we got there we were met by not one but three of Alfred's grandsons who showed us all round the farm.

What I took to be abandoned pieces of rusting farm machinery lying around the place were actually just waiting to be polished up and painted by Clive, who is reviving such traditional arts as ploughing with horses. We left him at the farm to get on with his work, and the two remaining brothers escorted Bill and myself to the house that Mary built, further up the village. It has since been divided into three dwellings, with the word 'farm' removed from its name: it is now Poplar House.

After all this house-inspecting Bill, one of whose missions on his short visit to England was to have a proper pub lunch, took me and the two brothers for a meal at the Spotted Dog. As we thanked the brothers for their kindness and their time, they handed me a folder full of photocopies of their grandfather's diaries. Then they looked at each other and said, 'there was something else, only we weren't sure we should tell you.' After a little prodding they explained that Alfred had had a bit of a falling out with Mary at the time of buying the house from her. I assured them I wanted to know everything, and they promised to send me the diary pages they'd kept back. I deposited Bill on the next train back to London, and took my precious keepsake home to pore over at leisure.

I was very moved by the contents of the folder. For one thing, Linden (the family historian) had gone to an extraordinary amount of effort photocopying every diary entry that mentioned Lady St Helier, marking the margins with green felt tip and typing out those that were hard to read. He had attached various pictures of both houses at different times, and other material such as an auctioneer's bill and the Collins' tenancy agreement. For another, Alfred kept his diary and accounts meticulously, offering a glimpse into a life that was by no means easy.

EPILOGUE

The Collins brothers in front of their 17th century farmhouse

Every day he recorded the weather – many entries start with 'Very nice day' – which cows were calving, which fields were mown or harrowed, and what vegetables were grown: oats, cabbage, potatoes and mangold wurzels (he calls them mangles). He employed a horseman, Sid, whom he paid £1 a week plus 4d an hour for overtime. Sid spent quite a lot of time mowing for Mary, as well as carting coal, logs and manure to her house. In April 1917 Alfred writes:

> Very bright sunny day – just the day for sowing, but unfortunately we had arranged to unload a truck of coal from Hermitage for Cloisters [a small religious community]. Sid did two journeys to their farm on the Long Lane Road and brought 1½ tons to Poplar Farm House. The mare kicked and broke shaft: cost more to repair than we earned all day.

Alfred also kept detailed accounts of produce he supplied to

Mary: milk (4d a pint), butter, apples, cream, potatoes, eggs (4½d each) and chickens. Sometimes he took vegetables and chickens to Newbury or Thatcham station to go up by train to her London house. From Alfred's diaries it appears that Mary did not spend very much time in the Cold Ash house, and quite often it was let to other people. She must have been too busy.

Alfred Collins with son Cyril on horse

In November of 1920 Mary offered the farmhouse to Alfred Collins to buy. A series of diary entries chart Alfred's tussle with Dreweatts, the local estate agents, over the course of the following year, as he wasn't sure he could afford it. He made an offer which was refused, and Mary sent another estate agent down from London to put pressure on him: 'when I got home was surprised to find a gentleman from Hamptons waiting to see me on the same subject… he wanted me to increase my offer.' Alfred refused.

In February 1921 he wrote asking Mary to relet the farm to him, but she did not want to do this, instead agreeing to the lower price. Now Alfred had cold feet: 'Did something which no doubt we shall regret decided not to buy the farm at the price asked.' Three days later he changed his mind and 'reluctantly decided to buy'. In September he took the plunge: 'paid a deposit to buy this farm am afraid it's a great mistake'. In December, just over a year after the start of negotiations, he completed and the farm was his. I hope that by the time three generations of Collins had been raised in the farmhouse he no longer felt it to be a mistake.

Following the sale there was a certain amount of bad blood between Alfred and his former landlady. They fell out over the cost of repairs to a pump which had taken place during the negotiating phase, she refusing to pay. This led to another chapter of wrangling, for Alfred was determined to get the money out of her. In October 1923 he 'called on Lady St Helier as she is leaving on Monday with reference to her long standing account, but she declined to see me.' Eighteen months later relations deteriorated further, as Alfred decided to take her to court, and in April 1925 records that 'Lady St Helier came to Poplar Farm House for Easter but told Mrs Isles [housekeeper?] not to have anything from us as we had put her into the County Court to obtain our owings.' In June, the evening before the court case, she settled the disputed account.

Was parsimony finally getting the better of the erstwhile champion of the poor? Or perhaps it was just old age making her cantankerous. Mary had another court case the year after she sold the farm, on a summons for rates arrears. When interviewed by a reporter, she was indignant.

> 'It is outrageous that such an advantage should be taken of what was a genuine slip of memory on my part. The payment of £33 4s 0d is due for the half-year's rates on my little cottage at Coldash, near Newbury. The summons did not reach in time, as I have been travelling, and the moment I heard of the money being due I sent off a cheque, which apparently arrived too late. I thought that the amount had been paid long ago, and I had actually put the accounts away. The smallness of the amount makes the affair almost ludicrous. However, all is settled now.'

Her chutzpah in describing a house big enough to divide into three dwellings as a 'little cottage' almost takes one's breath away…

Strange to say, my encounter with the Collins brothers brought me closer to my great-great-grandmother than the reams of accolades I'd read in the family album. It feels easier to relate, or be related, to someone when you know of their shortcomings.

Mary's death on 25th January 1931 provoked a flurry of obituaries in all the broadsheets and tabloids, all carefully pasted into albums by her daughter Dorothy. Some focused on her social work, others on her social circle. They shared a common theme – this one, lazily copied by several newspapers, feels like a good one to go out on:

> Her personality, it is true, was striking; yet it was by her amazing competence that she succeeded where others had failed. Her material advantages were not overwhelming. She was never a very wealthy woman, nor did she possess the outward trappings of a great position. And yet, in the last few years of the reign of Queen Victoria, she acquired a social prestige second to none.

I don't believe she ever craved recognition. The epitaph she chose for her grave, between Francis father and Francis son in Chieveley churchyard, reads simply: 'Wife and Mother'.

Appendix: The Curse of the Mackenzies

Back in the 17th century, Brahan Castle was inhabited by Kenneth Mackenzie, 3rd Earl of Seaforth. On his estate lived another Kenneth Mackenzie, a loyal worker prized for his gift of second sight, and better known as Coinneach Odhar (Brown Kenneth). The third person in this tale is a classic antiheroine: Lady Seaforth, a 'haughty woman of violent and jealous temper'.

When Lord Seaforth was away in Paris for an extended period of time his wife's suspicions grew hard to bear, and she sent for Coinneach to tell her what her husband was up to. The Seer held his white seeing-stone to his eye and assured Lady Seaforth that her husband was safe and well. His reluctance to say any more only made her more suspicious, and she would not let him leave until he divulged the whole picture. Under duress, Coinneach came out with this: 'Your lord is in a fair chamber hung with fine tapestry, and there is a bonnie lady with him, and he is on bended knees before her, with her hand pressed to his lips.'

It was just as she had thought. The rage of Lady Seaforth knew no bounds. Like many a recipient of bad news she turned on the messenger, branding him a slanderer and a witch, and ordered him to be taken to Chanonry Point, near Fortrose, to be burned to death in a barrel of tar. Before he was dragged away, however, Coinneach held the seeing-stone to his eye once more and uttered the following prophecy:

> I see into the far future, and I read there the doom of my destroyer. Ere many generations have passed, the line of Seaforth

will become extinct in sorrow. I see the last male of his line both deaf and dumb. I see his three fair sons, all of whom he will follow to their grave... A black-eyed lassie from the East, with snow on her coif, shall succeed him; she shall kill her sister; and she shall be the last of the Mackenzies of Seaforth.

A century went by, and sure enough a deaf and dumb Mackenzie, Mary's great-grandfather, was to be found living in Brahan Castle. Francis Humberston Mackenzie had contracted scarlet fever in childhood, and this had caused irreversible damage to his hearing, and thereby to his speech. He was known by the locals as MacCoinneach Bodhar, or Deaf Mackenzie. Although he could only communicate via pen and paper, his disability did not stop him from pursuing successful callings as a politician, colonial governor and amateur botanist. But, as the Seer had predicted, his sons died one after another, without producing any children.

The death of his final son in 1814 broke Francis Humberston both mentally and physically, and three months later he followed him to the grave. With this the title became extinct and the house of Seaforth was no more. Of Francis' ten children only two daughters remained, one of whom was Mary Frederica, Mary's grandmother. She now inherited the Brahan Estate.

But the story is not finished, for the second part of the prophecy was yet to be fulfilled. The 'black-eyed lassie from the East, with snow on her coif' was Mary Frederica herself. Her husband, Vice-Admiral Samuel Hood, had died in Madras on Christmas Eve in 1814, and she returned to Brahan wearing the white coif of mourning that was traditional in India. Because of this, or because of her married name, or both, she is generally known as 'the Hooded Lassie'. Walter Scott knew all about the curse on the family, for at the time he wrote to an acquaintance:

> Our friend Lady Hood will now be Caberfae [chieftain] herself. She has the spirit of a chieftainess in every drop of her blood, but

the estate is terribly embarrassed and will require great prudence in management… I do fear the accomplishment of the prophecy that when there should be a dumb Caberfae the house was to fall.

Mary Frederica Mackenzie was quite equal to the challenge of inheriting an 'embarrassed' estate. Within two years she married a James Stewart who added his name to hers, and used the proceeds from selling his own property to fund major improvements to the Castle. Things were looking up. Children came along, four in four years, but tragedy was waiting in the wings.

Mary Frederica's eldest boy Keith (Mary's father) was only five years old when, on the morning of 29th March 1823, she took her sister Caroline out in a little pony chaise along the West Drive. Suddenly the pony galloped out of control, and both sisters were thrown out into the ditch. Mary Frederica lost consciousness and awoke to see her sister standing in the road, dazed and spattered with blood. Caroline had severe head injuries, and in spite (or possibly because) of repeated bloodlettings and other ministrations by doctors from Dingwall, Inverness, and London, a month later she was dead. A monument to the accident was erected on the West Drive where it can be seen to this day, bearing a Latin inscription which translated says: 'At this point, according to the prophecy, Caroline Mackenzie, daughter of Francis, Lord Seaforth, was snatched from life.'

My intention is not to convince anyone of the authenticity of the Seer, but it is worth noting that his prophecies are still taken seriously in the Highlands. He is believed to have foreseen the advent of the railways and the Caledonian Canal. In Strathpeffer, not far from Brahan, stands the Eagle Stone, an ancient Celtic stone and the object of one of his predictions. If this stone should fall three times, said the Seer, the surrounding valley would flood and the stone would be used as an anchor for ships sailing up the valley. The stone has fallen twice, and in order to prevent a third collapse it has now been cemented in place by the local council.

But more to the point of this story is the continual shortage of heirs to the Brahan estate, as one after another they succumbed to early deaths, or simply failed to produce offspring. After Mary Frederica died, Keith Stewart Mackenzie moved to London. At some point he tried to sell off the estate, but Mary and her sister Julia took him to court and stopped him. After Keith's death Mary's brother Frank inherited, but a successful military career delayed his permanent move to Brahan.

On retirement he cleverly married Mary Steinkopf, whose father was the millionaire chairman of the Apollinaris mineral water company. (Hence she was known to the family as the 'appallin' heiress'.) Her wealth enabled her and Frank to live in the Castle in relative comfort to the end of their days, though by the time they married they were too old to have any children. Mary was the only member of the family who did, and next in line of succession would have been her son Francis – dead at 22.

In 1919 the *Aberdeen Press and Journal* said: 'The 'curse' of Seaforth is supposed to possess its malign force yet, and male heirs are not to be looked for in the family'. They were quite right. Dorothy's son Harry died at 23. This left Madeleine Brodrick's two boys. Uncanny coincidence, or power of the Seer? They were both killed within 24 hours of each other at Salerno, Italy, in WW2. Francis was 33, Michael 23. Neither had any children.

On the death of her cousins my grandmother, also a Madeleine, took on the estate and the name Stewart Mackenzie, but after fifteen years she decided to move back south for health reasons. Due to legalities too intricate for me to understand, let alone explain, no part of Brahan belonged to her, she was merely its custodian. Now the line of succession went back through one of Keith Stewart Mackenzie's sisters and ended up with the Matheson family, very distant relations.

Somewhere along the line the requirement to change your name to Stewart Mackenzie had evaporated, and with it, it seems, the power of Coinneach Odhar. Brahan has now housed four generations of Matheson men and boys, who through hard work and perseverance have turned the estate into a going concern. The curse, it seems, has been converted into a blessing.

A Succession of Females

Mary Stewart Mackenzie/Stanley/
Jeune/Lady St Helier

Dorothy Stanley/Allhusen

Madeleine Allhusen/Congreve/
Tyler/Stewart Mackenzie

Henrietta Congreve/Tyler

Amelia Tyler/Fletcher

Bibliography

Memories of 50 Years Lady St Helier (Edward Arnold 1909)

As We Were – a Victorian Peep-show EF Benson (Hogarth Press 1985)

The Ludovisi Goddess – Life of Louisa Lady Ashburton Virginia Surtees (Michael Russell 1984)

The Amberley Papers Ed. Bertrand and Patricia Russell (Norton 1937)

The Stanleys of Alderley: their Letters between the Years 1851-1865 Nancy Mitford (Chapman & Hall 1939)

The Criminal Conversation of Mrs Norton Diane Atkinson (Preface 2012)

Reminiscences – From the Table of my Memory Justin McCarthy (Harper & Bros 1899)

The Reminiscences of Lady Dorothy Nevill Ed. Ralph Nevill. (Thos. Nelson & Sons 1906)

Anglo-American Memories George W. Smalley (Duckworth 1912)

The Record of an Adventurous Life Henry Mayers Hyndman (Macmillan 1911)

The life of Henry George Henry George Jr (Doubleday Doran and Co 1900)

Selected Letters of Vernon Lee Mandy Gagel (Boston University 2008)

Many Celebrities and a few Others William H. Rideing (Eveleigh Nash, 1912)

The Blackest Streets Sarah Wise (Jonathan Cape 2008)

The True History of the Elephant Man Michael Howard & Peter Ford (Allison & Busby 1980)

Some Victorian Women, Good, Bad, and Indifferent Harry Furniss (Dodd Mead & Co New York 1923)
Marylebone Lives Ed. Mark Riddaway & Carl Upsall (Spiramus Press 2015)
Oscar Wilde, his Life and Confessions Frank Harris (1915)
My Life and Loves Frank Harris (Obelisk Press 1931)
Wilde's Women Eleanor Fitzsimons (Duckworth 2015)
The Modern Marriage Market ed. Marie Corelli (Hutchinson 1898)
The Collected Letters of Thomas Hardy Ed. by Michael Millgate (OUP 1978)
i myself Mrs T.P. O'Connor (G.P. Putnam's Sons 1914)
The Complete Motorist Filson Young (McClure/Philips/Methuen 1905)
My Early Life Winston Churchill (Butterworth 1930)
The River War Winston Churchill (Longmans 1899)
Fighting Mac: The Downfall of Major-General Sir Hector Macdonald Trevor Royle (Random House 2011)
The Life of the Rt. Hon. Sir Charles W. Dilke, Vol. 2 Stephen Gwynn (John Murray 1917)
Ida From Abroad Michelle Duster (BW Publishing 2001)
Lord Seaforth Finlay McKichan (Edinburgh University Press 2018)
Portrait of a Marriage Mary Soames (Paragon House 1987)
First Lady; the Life and Wars of Clementine Churchill Sonia Purnell (Aurum Press 2015)
Eminent Victorians Lytton Strachey (Bloomsbury 1988)
Correspondence of G.E. Morrison (CUP 1976)
The Letters of D.H. Lawrence Vol.2 Ed. Zytaruk &Boulton (CUP 1981)
The Open Air School Hugh Broughton (Sir Isaac Pitman & Sons 1914)
The Courage of the Early Morning William Arthur Bishop (McKay 1965)
Billy Bishop Goes to War John MacLachlan Gray & Eric Peterson (Talonbooks 1982)

Lesser Questions Lady Jeune (Remington and Co 1894)
The Diary of a Journalist Henry Lucy (John Murray 1920)
Letters of Sir Walter Scott Ed. HTC Grierson (London 1933)
'Converting Celebrity Status into Feminine Authority in the Periodical Press' Heather Weaver (dissertation)
https://marilyschwander.blogspot.com/search?q=mary+jeune

Mary Jeune's articles in chronological order

(LQ after the title denotes those collected into a single volume, *Lesser Questions*, 1894)

1885	Helping the Fallen *Fortnightly Review* (LQ)
	Saving the Innocents *Fortnightly Review* (LQ)
1887	Children of a Great City 1 & 2 *Woman's World*
1888	Irish Industrial Art *Woman's World*
	The Creed of the Poor *National Review* 11 (LQ)
	Technical Education for Women in England and Abroad *National Review* (LQ)
	Recollections of Mr Forster *National Review*
	A Highland Seer and Scotch Superstitions. *Murray's magazine* (LQ)
1889	Women of To-day, Yesterday, and To-morrow *National Review* (LQ)
	Competition and Co-operation among Women *English Illustrated Magazine*
	Children in Theatres *English Illustrated Magazine*
1890	Holidays for Poor Children *New Review*
	The Homes of the Poor *Fortnightly Review* (LQ)
	Children's Happy Evenings *English Illustrated Magazine*
1891	Anti-Humbug *National Observer* (aka The Salvation Army, LQ)
	Unfortunates: Reclaimables *National Observer*
	Unfortunates: Irreconcilables *National Observer*

	General Booth's Scheme *National Review*
1892	Brahan Castle (with Julia) *English Illustrated Magazine*
	LONDON SOCIETY *North American Review* (LQ)
	London Society and its critics *North American Review*
	The Servant Question *Fortnightly Review*
1893	Extravagance in Dress *National Review* (LQ)
	Amusements of the Poor *National Review*
	In Defence of the Crinoline *New Review* (LQ)
	The Poor Children's Holiday *Fortnightly Review*
	More about Society *The Pall Mall* magazine
1894	The Revolt of the Daughters *Fortnightly Review* (LQ)
	Where to spend a Holiday *Fortnightly Review*
	Dinners and Diners *North American Review* (LQ)
	An Englishwoman's Impressions of Ada Rehan *Harper's Weekly*
	Conversation in Society Illustrated by Phil May *English Illustrated Magazine* (LQ)
	The Domestic Servant *Lesser Questions*
1895	Cycling for Women *Badminton Magazine of Sports and Pastimes*
	English Women in Political Campaigns *North American Review*
	Political Great Ladies *The Realm*
	The Ideal Husband *Young Woman*
	A Rejoinder to London Society (3 articles) *Saturday Review*
	What is the Best Cycling Dress for Women? *The Woman at Home*
	The Ethics of Shopping *Fortnightly Review*
1896	What Christmas means to Queen Victoria *The Ladies' Home Journal*
	English Society as it is *Saturday Review*
	The Salon in England *Saturday Review*
1897	Early marriages: Should they be encouraged or abolished? *Idler*

	The Modern Marriage Market *Lady's Realm*
	The Duchess of Teck *The Contemporary Review*
1898	The New Woman and the Old: a Reply to Sarah Grand *Lady's Realm*
1899	Children and the State *Review of the Week*
1900	A Century of Women *Anglo-Saxon Review*
	The Decay of the Chaperon *Fortnightly Review*
	The American Spirit in British Society *Saturday Evening Post*
1901	The Art of Entertaining *Cosmopolitan*
	The Future of Society *Lady's Realm*
	Some Aspects of Modern Society *New Liberal Review*
	Victoria and Her Reign *North American Review*
	Woman: some phases and crazes *Gentlewoman: Old and New Century* (Quoted in *Eve's Century: A Sourcebook of Writings on Women and Journalism 1895-1950*, edited by Anne Varty)
1902	The New Influence on the British Throne *North American Review*
	Dress for Ladies *Badminton Library of Sports and Pastimes: Motoring*
	Entry on 'Women' for *Encyclopaedia Britannica*
1904	The Social Side of Motoring *The Complete Motorist* Filson Young
1907	The Athletic Woman *Ladies' Field*
1909	London Society in the Sixties *Harper's Monthly Magazine*
	Worthy Work for Young Ladies *The Quiver*
1911	The Training of English Children *Century Magazine*
1916	Kitchener: England's Man of Iron *Harper's Magazine* 133
1919	The chaperon's return *Telegraph*

Acknowledgements

Besides my sister Camilla, who has been my most staunch supporter and helpmeet in this project over the last several years, I would like to thank the following people. Bill Davis, for his fondness for Mary Jeune and for providing me with a comprehensive collection of her essays. Sarah Wise, for finding out things I never knew about her and would otherwise never have known. Peter Buckman for his faith in me, his enthusiasm for the book, and a lunch. The Collins brothers, for the contents of the Epilogue.

Any inaccuracies are entirely my fault.

Picture credits

Hyndman: Emery Walker, Public domain, via Wikimedia Commons

Chamberlain: Elliott & Fry, Public domain, via Wikimedia Commons

Tichborne trial: Hampshire County Council. Provided by the Hampshire Cultural Trust, 2025

Ida B. Wells: Cihak and Zima, Public domain, via Wikimedia Commons

Billy Bishop: National Archives of Canada: PA-122514

The Collins family: Daniel Collins